UNBREAK THE SYSTEM

UNBREAK
THE SYSTEM

Diagnosing and Curing the
Ten Critical Flaws in Your Company

JOSH ROVNER

LIONCREST
PUBLISHING

UNBREAK THE SYSTEM

Diagnosing and Curing the Ten Critical Flaws in Your Company

ISBN   978-1-5445-0571-8 *Hardcover*
       978-1-5445-0569-5 *Paperback*
       978-1-5445-0570-1 *Ebook*

CONTENTS

INTRODUCTION... 7

TROUBLE AFTER SCHOOL 13

FLAWS

POLITICS 33

BLIND SPOTS 63

SCAPEGOATING 95

UNCLEAR GOALS... 119

DOING TOO MUCH..147

DYSFUNCTIONAL INFRASTRUCTURE.............. 161

NO SOPs..183

FIXING THE UNFIXABLE....................................... 213

LEGACY TECHNOLOGY 227

CHASING SHINY OBJECTS 245

AN OUNCE OF PREVENTION 263

CONCLUSION...269

ACKNOWLEDGMENTS 275

ABOUT THE AUTHOR..279

INTRODUCTION

It's that time again.

You just got the P&L from last quarter.

You jump right to the bottom line.

Down compared to last year.

Same thing the quarter before. And the quarter before that, even though the results were slightly up compared to last year, you didn't hit your budget. You felt pressure to do better.

It's hard to keep coming up with new ideas for how to improve. There's a lot going on.

You know you're about to be under the gun. You think about the first question you're going to be asked. You know what it is.

The first question everyone is going to ask you is: Why are we down?

* * *

Sound familiar?

Of course, you're going to give them an explanation. But it's going to be superficial.

You'll call it "high level." But really that just means you don't know for sure—or there are too many variables, and you had to come up with a few key areas you think will satisfy them.

You've tried a lot of different initiatives, but they haven't driven the results you need. You know that underneath the superficial explanation of "market segment A and revenue stream B are down," there is something else you can't put your finger on that's holding back your company's performance.

In order to do better, you know your company needs to change. And it needs to change fast. But that's just not happening.

You may think the reason your company is struggling is because there's something wrong with your culture. But that's not it. And you don't have bad people either, even if you think you might.

What you have is a broken system created by common but critical flaws. These flaws exist all around you, working together like a bad infection to hold your company back and kill it.

You can feel them and the symptoms they create. They cause pain for you, your employees, your customers, your shareholders, and all of your families. Yet they're invisible.

They're what you can't put your finger on.

Until now.

HOW THIS BOOK CAN HELP YOU

This book is a radically different approach to transforming your company.

This book is about changing your company's situation.

Because when you change the situation, everything else follows. From that entirely new situation comes the improved financial performance you are so desperately seeking.

This book explores the ten critical flaws in companies that lie under the surface to kill performance. The flaws are universal. Fixing them does not require experience in your industry or a deep understanding of your business.

The ten critical flaws are:

- Politics

- Blind Spots

- Scapegoating

- Unclear Goals

- Doing Too Much

- Dysfunctional Infrastructure

- No Standard Operating Procedures (SOPs)

- Fixing the Unfixable

- Legacy Technology

- Chasing Shiny Objects

This book will help you understand these critical flaws. It

will teach you how to identify them in your company and what you can do to get rid of them.

I've discovered these flaws based on twenty-plus years working in corporate America. I've held positions at many levels, from unpaid intern to middle management to senior leadership. I've been a business leader directly responsible for financial results, and I've been a consultant. My background is in management and leadership, learning and development, communications, organizational effectiveness, human performance improvement, and process improvement. I've experienced what it's like to be held back by these critical flaws. I've seen what happens in companies when they take hold and when they are corrected.

I want to share the flaws with you and help you cure them, so you don't allow them to stay hidden in the shadows, quietly killing you and your company.

I hope this book will help you see things in a new way and enable you to change your approach to how you run your company. By doing so, not only will you be better prepared to answer the question, "Why are we down?", but you may improve your results so much that you never have to answer that question again.

TROUBLE AFTER SCHOOL

I once worked with a company that provided after-school care for young children. As part of the program, there was dedicated time when the kids were supposed to do their homework. And yet, very few of the kids actually would.

Instead, they would all get up out of their chairs and start talking to their friends, which was very noisy, and which they were not supposed to do (and they knew they were not supposed to do it, but they did it anyway).

The program staff decided that the kids were "rule breakers." So they decided to give them assigned seats, both as a punishment and to prevent them from talking to their friends, which was always too loud and disruptive. They also asked teachers (who were not part of the after-school program) if they could give the kids more homework. That way, they thought, the kids would be busier and not have time to goof off.

But the teachers said they couldn't do that. They were already giving the maximum amount of homework allowable. The situation did not improve.

The company leaders told me about the problem. I organized a meeting for a few days later with all the people involved. My first question was, "Why aren't the kids doing their homework?"

"They just have a lot of attitude, and they don't want to listen," the program leader told me.

"Have you ever asked any of them why they don't do their homework?" I asked. Blank stare. No answer. Obviously not.

So we brought in one girl, who the leader said was "one of the better ones." After establishing with the girl that she does her homework at home once she leaves the after-school program, I said to her, "Help me understand. Are you saying that you avoid doing your homework here even though you have plenty of time to do it? And instead you choose to do it at home when you could do any number of other things that are more fun?"

"Uh-huh," she said.

Here's how the rest of the conversation went:

Me: So why don't you do your homework in the time that's allowed during the after-school program, especially if that's what you're supposed to do?

Girl: Because it's way too noisy in the room. I can't concentrate at all.

Me: OK. Well, that makes sense. So what do you do instead of doing your homework?

Girl: Well, I usually just sit there. But sometimes I also go talk to my friends, and sometimes I get in trouble for that.

The after-school program leader was stunned at the girl's answer. Her reason had never occurred to her.

I recognized, in the words of Chip and Dan Heath, authors of the great book *Switch: How to Change Things When Change is Hard*, "what looks like a people problem is actually a situation problem."

I turned to the leader and asked, "Have you ever thought about what you can do to make the after-school room quieter? Or potentially give the kids a quieter place to do their homework?"

Immediately, the teachers and the program leader started brainstorming. And they found lots of ways to fix the situation. Working together with the school teachers, the program leader was able to secure a different classroom for the kids who wanted to do their homework quietly.

For the kids who didn't have homework, or once they were finished with homework, this was another problem. According to the program leader, they didn't want to play with the games the staff had provided. The leader rattled off all the games they had put out for the kids.

And then she said, scornfully, "We give them all these games, and yet they just won't play with them."

Once again, I knew that the issue was not the kids even though she was framing it that way. It was the situation. The environment. The games. The games were not fun for the kids even though the program leader thought they were fun.

I asked the girl, "Why don't you and the other kids play with the games?"

"I guess we just don't think they're that fun."

"What games do you like to play?" I asked. The girl named a few.

And bang. The program leader and the teachers in the

room lit up. They said they could easily get those games—and they thought of several more, which the girl agreed were "cool." They talked about how the kids could easily play the games with their friends in groups, which both the leader and all the teachers said was a great thing.

"Wait a minute," I said to the leader. "I thought you said you didn't want kids talking to their friends. Aren't you worried that the volume is going to be too loud if they are playing games with their friends?"

Both she and the teachers jumped in immediately. "Oh, no," they said. "When they are playing an appropriate game with their friends, then the noise level is fine. It's only bad when they're just socializing with their friends and don't have anything to focus on."

"So then do they really need assigned seats?" I asked. "I mean, if you're saying that the problem is not actually talking to their friends but, really, it's talking to their friends in an unfocused, purely social way, then it doesn't seem like having assigned seats away from their friends really has anything to do with the problem. In fact, it seems like it might be causing other problems—like kids getting up out of their seats to go talk to their friends. You said that's a problem, too, because the kids often 'give you attitude' when you tell them to go back to their seats and stop talking to their friends."

"Wow," the leader said. "I never really thought of that."

After the meeting, the program leader decided to take away the assigned seats and allow the kids to sit with their friends when they weren't doing homework. She and her staff made sure to give them fun games that the kids liked that allowed them to play with their friends in a group. This actually helped the kids focus and learn, which was the real goal of the after-school program. And it kept the noise level reasonable.

With these few tweaks, everything about the environment and the success of the after-school program changed. That change cut through the politics and animosity between the program leaders and the teachers. Previously, some of the kids who originally weren't doing homework would wander the halls inappropriately, which led the teachers to believe that the after-school program staff were incompetent, while at the same time the after-school staff thought the teachers were just trying to cause them trouble.

Just by meeting together as we did, the program leader and the school teachers were able to show each other that they really do want the same things and that they respect and support each other. They also got buy-in from the girl we involved, who agreed to be a champion to help her friends do better.

Notice that these significant changes did not take any "large-scale change management initiatives." They did not take putting the staff through leadership development programs. There was no additional training necessary. And none of the people changed.

All these changes came from one simple meeting, properly facilitated, with the right people in the room, that lasted less than an hour. And all the "problems" the program was dealing with previously were really symptoms that had been caused by clear misdiagnosis and clear mistreatment.

Obviously, not every problem in your company may be that easy. You may be saying, "I'm a top executive at a major company. What does this have to do with me? This is a story about kids, schools, and academic organizations. That's not my industry. That's not my business. Those aren't my people."

But you're wrong. Your company's situation is really very similar to this. As Bob Pike, a pioneer in the training world, says, "Adults are babies with big bodies." And the after-school program company was a for-profit company with many stakeholders, just like yours.

LESSONS LEARNED AFTER SCHOOL AND FROM THE DOCTOR

Let's look at the general lessons this story gives us that you need to apply when you are working through the critical flaws in your company. We'll look at the doctor/patient relationship as well, because it's a very helpful framework when dealing with your critical flaws, which are very much like a disease in your company.

DIAGNOSE PROPERLY

Just as with the story above, and just like any successful doctor/patient relationship, turning things around in your company starts with a proper diagnosis. Without proper diagnosis, you may apply the wrong treatment. If you misdiagnose and apply the wrong treatment in your company, no one will actually die, but the problem will continue.

Not only will you not solve your problem, but, like the story above—or like a doctor giving the wrong medicine to a patient—you may cause other problems. You may do any or all of the following:

- Create new problems that didn't exist before

- Exacerbate existing problems

- Break a process that's working

- Waste peoples' time that doesn't need to be wasted

- Spend money where there is no ROI

TREAT DIRECTLY AND AGGRESSIVELY

One of the best pieces of advice when dealing with a critical flaw is to make sure you hit it head-on with direct and aggressive treatment. If your doctor has diagnosed you with a bacterial infection that could really harm you, he or she will give you appropriate antibiotics to treat the particular type of infection you have. Your doctor will choose the best and most direct treatment for your condition to ensure you get better as quickly as possible with as few side effects as possible.

In the Trouble After School story, I worked quickly to ask proper questions that got to the root of the problem, which was actually the situation and environment (the noise in the room; the boring games), and then guided the program leader and the teachers to treat those problems directly and aggressively.

Of course, if you have complex underlying conditions, your doctor will take those into account and may need to vary the treatment somewhat because of that. But otherwise, whatever is the most direct and aggressive treatment is what's ideal.

The same thing is true when dealing with flaws in an organization. Yes, it's important to consider the nuances of what the organization does, how it's structured, and so on. But otherwise, it's best to hit the flaws head-on through direct and aggressive treatment.

GATHER ALL PARTIES

As part of the direct and aggressive treatment of a company flaw, you need to bring it up to the person or people who are primarily responsible for it. If the problem involves a group of people (and especially if that group includes you and your direct team, which it probably does), get them together to talk it out. Make sure everyone who is part of the issue is in the room.

It's best to do this in person in a meeting, not on a conference call, which is generally very distracting. Although it can be difficult to get everyone together, and it may cost money to have everyone in a meeting, it is worth it. Not having everyone in the room means that someone can knowingly or unknowingly sabotage progress after the fact.

All the parties in the after-school program who had a hand in the matter were in the room together. That was very intentional. If I hadn't done it that way, we would not have been able to solve the issue as quickly and effectively as we did.

The issue would have festered and gotten worse. The perspective of the girl would have been lost. And once there was communication among the parties, it probably would have been an endless stream of back-and-forth accusatory emails that worsened the politics and tensions.

INVOLVE OUTSIDE FACILITATORS AND/OR COACHES

Usually, critical flaws are too substantial to deal with internally only, and often even HR isn't skilled enough or neutral enough to address them properly. You need an effective outside facilitator or coach guiding you through the process. You will probably need multiple facilitators and coaches at certain points.

Sometimes it's good to have facilitators with a background in industrial/organizational psychology. But be careful that they don't get caught up in too much theory or that they only try to focus on leadership development or something else that addresses the people but not the situation.

It can be particularly helpful to have people who have degrees in counseling—especially for the times when you have to deal with highly sensitive topics like politics—because they understand peoples' emotions and how to really help them make meaningful change (note that this is very different from corporate "Change Management").

It's also critical that the outside facilitators and coaches you work with understand business. They don't have to be in your industry, but they should understand business well. Ideally, they've worked in the business world and have "seen a thing or two."

I volunteered to facilitate the after-school meeting when I heard about the after-school company's problem. The fact that I was not part of the problem, yet I understood the situation, business in general, and how to deal with peoples' emotions while just focusing on the situation, was very helpful and allowed the main parties to focus on solutions.

COMMUNICATE TO OTHERS OUTSIDE THE ROOM

Especially if the process to fix the critical flaws in your company takes time, which it will, make sure to communicate to others outside the core team what you and the group are doing and have done to fix the flaws and how that will impact them moving forward. Admit that the flaws were causing others problems and holding the organization back. It's OK to give some details, as long as it doesn't violate confidentiality.

As a way to model good communication, talk through the process you used or are using to solve the problem with those outside the room.

CONDUCT A FOLLOW-UP VISIT IF NECESSARY

If you go to the doctor with a simple sinus infection and you get better after a short course of antibiotics, there's no need to go back to the doctor just to say you're better. But in some cases, if the illness you have is really bad, you may need to go back to get follow-up tests or examinations to make sure you are better. Same thing with your company. Once the flaws are addressed, follow up to measure whether the symptoms are better. It's quite possible, though, that you won't even need a formal follow-up. By going through this diagnostic and treatment process, the company's financial results will naturally begin to improve, people will naturally behave differently, and everyone will naturally notice and feel the difference.

No follow-up was necessary at the school. The situation improved itself after the meeting, and the after-school program leader and teachers both told me shortly thereafter that everything was much better.

There are many ways to formally measure whether your critical flaws are cured. These include financial metrics of your company, customer satisfaction surveys, employee engagement surveys, and so on. My website, www.joshrovner.com, contains some great resources as well.

But even with all the options for objective measures, don't underestimate the value of how the company "feels."

More than likely, you will know more quickly whether the company is better just by how you feel each day.

ADDITIONAL LESSONS

In addition to the lessons described above, there are a few other things to discuss about the critical flaws and about getting the most out of this book and the treatment process.

TREAT ALL YOUR FLAWS

One of the biggest questions people ask when I talk about critical flaws in a company is: Can a company have more than one critical flaw at the same time? In a word, yes. In two words, hell yes.

Most companies that are struggling with poor performance have multiple critical flaws. And they are all connected, as you will see.

If you want to fix your company's performance, you must treat all the flaws, and you must treat them each thoroughly and completely. If you don't, you risk a recurrence. Or your problems may never really go away. It's like stopping antibiotics two days into a ten-day course because you have started to feel better. It's a really bad idea that could make your flaws and company performance worse.

And then you might blame me, which I don't want! Especially since that's just scapegoating, which is one of the critical flaws you'll learn about.

I once worked with a client who didn't treat all the flaws and implement all the actions we discussed. What was really a shame was that his organization had made so much progress after we started. It slipped back when he stopped moving forward with the process in order to chase a shiny object that was a total distraction. He concluded the lack of further improvement was because the treatment process was the problem.

I'm not saying this approach is perfect. No way. I've made tons of mistakes in my life, and I know there are many things I could have done differently with the process—even in this situation. But the treatment wasn't the problem with this one. The problem was that he chose to stop the antibiotics two days in. You can't blame the doctor if you are a non-compliant patient.

USE YOUR RESOURCES

In order to help you on this journey, and it is a journey, there are a lot of resources available to you on my website. Take advantage of them, particularly the Action Plan Template. I recommend completing this as you read through the book. It's a good idea to have it with you whenever you read the book—and, ideally, all the time (either in digital form or on paper—whatever works best for you).

Great, hard-to-achieve results almost never happen without proper planning and preparation, so skip this step at your peril. Plus, you never know when, after reading something, you will have an epiphany or remember something you want to do and wish to write it down in your action plan.

If you complete your action plan as you read, then once you've finished the book, you will have a solid, ready-to-use "playbook" that you can immediately execute from to start curing the critical flaws in your company.

I also highly recommend filling out the Company Symptom Questionnaire (available on my website) right after you finish the book. It will really help you see the whole picture, and it will provide a great comparison benchmark after treatment to validate whether your flaws have been cured or not.

HAVE PATIENCE, GIVE IT TIME, INVEST A LITTLE

I know you want to fix everything quickly. If you work through the critical flaws as discussed here, you will start to see progress soon. Some things will be fast and easy to handle. But don't think that this process is some quick fix magic bullet. It's not, and it may take some money to help you get through everything. But it doesn't have to be a whole lot.

Most of the solutions I present in this book do not cost a lot of money. Some may cost a bit more, but they will be worth it. Just realize that curing critical flaws is not something you can solve simply by throwing money at it.

TIME TO START

Now that I've set the stage for you, it's time to get started with diagnosing and curing your company's critical flaws.

Don't worry. Getting started is easy. In fact, it's the easiest thing you'll do in the journey and probably the easiest thing you will do today.

All you have to do is turn the page. Let's jump right in.

FLAWS

POLITICS

The facilitator flipped his pen anxiously as he waited for someone to speak up. Twelve people in the room, and no one said a word.

Everyone shifted uncomfortably in their chairs and glanced quickly at the others, looking to see whether anyone would break the silence. No one did.

"Come on, guys..." the facilitator said. "We talked about this. It's okay to be honest."

Everyone did their best to avoid looking at the facilitator. Everyone hoped he wouldn't start calling on them.

They knew it wasn't really okay to be honest. Their boss was a political animal who would think nothing of getting rid of them, or, worse, keeping them and continuing to torture them—kind of like Kevin Spacey's character in the movie *Horrible Bosses*, only slower, steadier, and less dramatic.

They were acting like abused children, scared that their dad would find out what they said and let them have it. But they weren't children. They weren't even low-level employees. They were all highly paid, highly experienced corporate leaders. Their boss was one of the top executives in the company.

He had been told that he needed to soften his approach, so he arranged for the facilitator, as part of a team meeting, to get feedback from his direct reports about what he does poorly and what he could do better. But he'd been through this before. Even though he said he wanted to change, he really didn't. Everybody knew that.

Yet there they were, being asked to tattle on their boss. In public. As a group.

This leads to the first rule of dealing with politics: don't expect honest feedback in a group setting—especially if you are a "career politician" with direct authority over the people you're seeking feedback from!

I start with politics because it is one of the toughest flaws to tackle. Solving politics involves dealing with difficult emotions—probably the most difficult emotions we have as people. And that naturally can be uncomfortable.

It is often particularly difficult for high-level executives like you, who are used to making rational decisions every day based on analysis and data in order to grow revenue, profit, or market share—all of which are supremely logical and devoid of emotion.

In addition to being one of the toughest problems to tackle, politics is also one of the most dangerous critical flaws. It causes all sorts of other problems throughout the organization and prevents focus on what really matters.

Deal with politics even though you don't want to. If you are trying to pretend that politics don't exist in your company, then stop. Because they do.

If you think you can ignore them and hope they will go away if you have everyone focus on this year's or this quarter's company goal, you're wrong. In that case, they are probably the reason the goal is not getting accomplished.

And the scariest but most important point you need to hear about politics: you're involved, whether you like it or not. In fact, you might even be the reason they're happening, especially if you have used or are currently using them to your advantage. If so, stop. Even if it doesn't seem

like it, politics are doing your company—and you—much
more harm than good.

FORMS OF POLITICS

Like the flu, there are a lot of different forms of politics—
so many that it's impossible to discuss them all here. But
I have a list of the top ten most virulent "strains" that
commonly occur in companies. They are:

1. **Hidden agendas**

2. **Exclusive inner circles**

3. **CYA culture**

4. **Tiptoeing**

5. **Finger pointing**

6. **Hidden bureaucracy**

7. **Bureaucratic immunity**

8. **Skip-level directions**

9. **Grass-roots implementation**

10. **Micromanagement**

Below is an examination of each one.

HIDDEN AGENDAS

This is when certain people or groups of people deliberately do things that are self-serving but don't really help the organization. Hidden agendas can come from people who may only want to promote themselves or their departments. Or they may come from people who are trying to make others look bad to take the focus off of them or their department when they know that they or their department are not doing well. Think about who in your company may have a hidden agenda that's causing an issue. Also, look in the mirror: what agendas are you hiding?

EXCLUSIVE INNER CIRCLES

If a leader has a small, close inner circle that excludes others knowingly or unknowingly—especially if the excluded people are part of the formal organizational structure—this causes a lot of fear and inefficiency. Even worse, I've seen senior leaders whose inner circles include people two or three levels down in the organization—people who report to their direct reports or report to the direct reports of their direct reports.

I'm not saying that inner circles are all bad. Almost every senior leader has one. Leaders can't do it alone. You need people you can truly trust to help you and help advance the organization.

But sometimes the inner circle can be more like a high school clique, and that's bad—especially if it includes people who are not your direct reports or excludes one or more of your direct reports. Often, this happens because you don't truly trust one of your direct reports. If that's the case, though, it's not productive to tiptoe around the issue.

Bob, Dave, and Jimmy

In one example I've seen, Bob, a senior vice president who reported to Dave, the CEO, didn't have a close relationship with Dave. But Jimmy, a vice president who reported to Bob, did.

Bob would provide direction to his team. But then Jimmy would tell the team a different direction because that's what Dave, the CEO, really wanted (which Jimmy learned while playing golf with Dave when Bob was not invited to play golf with Dave).

This dynamic between Bob, Jimmy, and Dave happened a lot. All the conflicting directions and the "dancing" around the strategy caused a lot of extra work for people in the organization, who never really knew exactly what was expected of them.

There was no alignment on direction because of politics at the higher levels. Since there was no clear direction (and, in fact, there were often conflicting directions), people were constantly getting in trouble because following one leader's direction violated the direction of another leader.

Bill, Steve, and Fred

Bill, a mid-level manager who reported to Steve, a vice president, had a close relationship with Steve's boss, Fred, who was a senior vice president. Bill was a long-standing employee of the company and had worked closely with Fred when the company was very small, so the two were very friendly.

Not only did Fred regularly bypass Steve to ask Bill's opinion about Steve's function and division; at one point, Fred even invited Bill to accompany him on an international trip that he should have invited Steve to—and did so without telling Steve.

Steve found out from Bill (his direct report) when one day Bill said, "Hey, I don't know if you heard about this, but Fred just invited me on this trip, so I think I need to go. That means that, two weeks from now, I will be out of the office for a week." Steve was stunned, but he had to let Bill go with Fred.

Even though it's fine for you to periodically check in with and form relationships with mid-level employees, you should not use it as a way to avoid having to deal with an uncomfortable political situation. Senior leaders in particular need to bring their direct reports into the "inner circle" if they aren't there already—or let them go if that's what's really necessary.

CYA CULTURE

In this version of politics, ideas, initiatives, or reports take a long time to get approved and have to go through multiple committees and approvals before they are implemented. No one wants to be guilty of making a mistake.

People know that making a mistake is not tolerated and will be met with harsh consequences. Those consequences could be as extreme as being fired. But it's also possible that won't happen, and instead, the people who make mistakes will just be belittled or discredited in some way.

That's also very painful—almost more painful than being

fired, in some cases, because those people then need to show up and face their belittlers every day. At a minimum, that consequence is painful enough to make people avoid it, which is why they work as hard as they can to cover themselves.

While you may feel that a true consensus has been achieved coming out of a committee, that may not be the case. True consensus (which is genuine agreement on a difficult decision) is not the same as CYA consensus. There is a parallel here to Chris Voss's great book on negotiating called *Never Split the Difference*. Voss explains that there is such a thing as a "counterfeit yes." A counterfeit yes occurs when someone outwardly agrees with you just to shut you up and get out of the interaction without having a conflict. They know they can't solve the conflict because you are unwilling to listen and negotiate.

Often in organizations that have CYA culture, what seems like true consensus is actually CYA consensus, similar to a counterfeit yes. If things go wrong, then CYA consensus turns into finger-pointing and blaming other people or groups. It becomes a hidden quest to make sure you or your department has its ass covered and doesn't "get egg on its face." Anyone or any department that does take the blame will have their reputation, credibility, and influence suffer.

Of course, this sounds ridiculous and horrible. It is obviously a very inefficient and ineffective way to operate. But it happens all the time. It's probably happening in your company.

CYA culture causes people to do things solely based on fear, which is not ideal. Yes, it's true that sometimes fear can be a good thing and help you focus. But not in this case, because the fear is artificially created and expanded beyond what is rational and appropriate for the situation.

There has been a lot of research showing that people don't make the best decisions when they are unnecessarily afraid. In order to make the best decisions for the most complex circumstances, we need our rational brains, which don't stay in the driver's seat when we're operating from fear.

Einstein said, "We cannot solve our problems with the same thinking we used when we created them." Making decisions based on CYA culture is not going to solve the company's problems. The CYA culture needs to be dealt with and removed in order for the company to operate with its rational brain, turn performance around, and advance to greatness.

TIPTOEING

Another type of politics is when people spend a lot of

time trying to tweak their ideas to conform to what one particular leader will accept or want to hear even if there are better ways. Everyone knows the leader won't accept the better ways because he or she is being irrational or stubborn.

Stuart

I knew a company that measured each unit's performance based on its market share. Each unit had to pick its competitors so the market share information was reported appropriately. Which competitors should be included was often a matter of debate because there were many possible competitors, but not all of them could be included for benchmarking purposes.

Several layers of people decided on the official competitive set for each unit. They included people who worked in the unit (who had the best knowledge of the competitive situation), as well as the corporate support team for that unit. Ultimately, however, the division president, Stuart, had the final approval. Stuart was notorious for not allowing a unit to change its competitive set once it was established. He always looked at this as a "play" to artificially make the requesting unit's market share performance look better—and nothing more.

On this occasion, the unit's employees and the corporate support team all agreed that the competitive set was wrong and made no sense. It included several competitors that were too far away and didn't have the same type of products or services. In fact, no one knew how the existing competitive set had been established originally. In spite of the fact that everyone agreed the competitive set needed to be changed (and there were multiple lengthy conversations about this), the change never happened.

At first, the discussion with Stuart was delayed (multiple times) because the corporate support team knew that it wouldn't sit well with him. When it was brought up, Stuart (unsurprisingly) said no to the change request without even looking at the proposal—even though everyone else was in complete and strong agreement that the change needed to happen, and the team had created a business case with appropriate justification.

Meanwhile, the unit continued to lose market share based on the imperfect competitive set. This caused the company to spend thousands of dollars trying to fix the issue. In reality, if the competitive set had been correct, the unit may have already shown the strongest market share, and that money could have been used for other, better purposes with much higher ROI.

Failure Is Not an Option

Another example of tiptoeing around irrational leaders is a company culture that does not truly accept failure. By accepting failure, I don't just mean giving it lip service, as many leaders do. I mean that leaders truly acknowledge (publicly and privately) that failure is okay. They ensure that people are not punished, ridiculed, or fired for failing if their effort was a sincere attempt to help the company and it just didn't work.

When you as a senior executive do not accept failure, people will go to great lengths to avoid presenting failure to you because they know you may react harshly. They will tiptoe around the issue even when it is crystal clear that something has failed. In this situation, middle or upper management will say to their teams, "We can't show the C-suite Executives that this pilot didn't actually work. We need to keep analyzing the numbers and the situation until we figure it out. We have to show something positive."

This leads to an incredible amount of extra, pointless work, as well as lots of stress and frustration. The stress is for the people doing the work, who worry that their failures will cause them harm. The frustration is not only for the people doing the work but also for you and your executive team, who are often misled by your teams into thinking something that already failed could actually work. Then, when it doesn't, there is frustration (and finger-pointing, of course).

As a high-level executive in your company, be aware that people may be doing these things because of you. If you think or know that may be happening, take steps to fix it.

FINGER-POINTING

Finger-Pointing is when certain people blame others for failure or certain departments blame other departments. This happens a lot in many organizations. It is never helpful.

While it is okay to examine the content and method of a process that involves a certain person or department and point out problems that legitimately need to be solved, it is very bad to simply make blanket statements about the person or department, as in "If the sales team wasn't so lazy and just did their job right, we wouldn't have this problem!"

Instead, focus on what the sales team didn't do and why they didn't do it. Chances are there is a situational or environmental "hill" standing in the way of the sales team that you need to change. (More on this in the chapter on Scapegoating.)

HIDDEN BUREAUCRACY

You obviously know what bureaucracy is. Hidden bureaucracy is a variation that happens when certain people or departments spontaneously "invent" bureaucracy to avoid accountability or looking bad.

I once knew a person who worked in a company where IT was a critical function that supported a service business. In this example, leaders from the service business agreed with the IT liaison in a meeting that a particular, simple piece of functionality needed to be designed into the system that supported the service.

After they agreed in the meeting, the business leads from the service organization assumed that everything was beginning for the development as agreed. They scheduled a status update for three weeks later.

Three weeks later, in the status update meeting, the business leads asked for the update. They were dumbfounded when the IT liaison said she hadn't started the project even though everyone had agreed in the last meeting that development would start. When asked why, she said, "Because you guys never filled out my form."

Of course, the business leads were furious—especially because this ridiculously small issue that never really existed could have easily been solved with a simple follow-up email if there actually had been a "form" to fill out. When they raised this concern and tried to get the bureaucracy dealt with, it made no real impact, and the bureaucratic faults of the IT department remained in place. It took many months for development work to start.

Certainly, this hurt the company's performance because the functionality would have made the service business more effective. But the real issue is that, in spite of all the complaints, the IT leader was not willing to face the fact that his IT organization had become a bureaucracy and was not functioning well. He just allowed it to continue.

BUREAUCRATIC IMMUNITY

Continuing with the IT/service business story, there was no way anyone could get the situation changed because, in spite of being completely ineffective, the IT leader had a lot of political power in the C-suite. He had "bureaucratic immunity."

Other department leaders, as well as the middle management who had to deal with this situation, used to joke that he "must have pictures of the CEO with farm animals." It wound up being a sad, sick joke. Whenever this type of situation happened, which was often, the victims would look at each other, shake their heads, and say, "farm animals!"

As a high-level leader in your company, make sure that no one thinks someone has pictures of you with farm animals.

SKIP-LEVEL DIRECTIONS

This happens when high-level executives give front line staff or lower-level staff direction or projects to work on without communicating clearly and directly to their supervisors, managers, or department heads. As a result, middle managers have to spend a lot of time chasing their direct reports because they don't know what their direct reports have been directed to do or how that direction may affect the rest of the workload.

Ironically, this type of thing often happens when senior leaders don't want to bother with the bureaucracy that they themselves preside over and may even have created. Or it could be an issue with specific people. It should be dealt with swiftly and directly, but often it isn't because of politics or an unwillingness for senior leaders to have honest conversations.

Skip-level directions not only delay work; they also make people feel uncomfortable and awkward. Think about how you would feel if the board told one of your direct report leaders to do something that interfered with the initiatives you asked the person to work on, and did it without telling you.

Now think about if you were the one who got the request. Even as a high-level executive, it would feel very awkward to have to tell your boss (or hide) what the situation is when he or she should have known first.

When this stuff happens over and over again, it leads to a culture of disengagement, inefficiency, and ineffectiveness. Trust goes out the window as people realize that they now have to start paying attention to politics. That holds the organization back in huge, deep ways that can be difficult to measure but are easy to "feel."

GRASS-ROOTS IMPLEMENTATION

Sometimes skip-level politics manifest themselves in programs that seem like they are legitimate and helpful but really are fueled by hidden politics. I've worked with many companies that have implemented "leadership development" or "leadership training"—including many who have it as an ongoing function.

Fearful of upsetting higher-level leaders or having to get higher-level leaders to truly change how they operate, someone (usually HR) will start to implement these programs at the lowest supervisory level. They justify it by saying that the supervisors are the ones who need the programs the most because they are younger and new to "leadership" in general.

While this can certainly be true in some cases and is definitely valid for some parts of leadership, it ignores the fact that low-level supervisors operate in an environment that's shaped by the higher-level leaders—including the highest-level leaders.

It is well known that corporate culture emanates from the top down, even if that doesn't sound popular these days. Trying to change the culture and improve an organization's performance by doing a "grass-roots" campaign is not the way to go. But it often happens because no one is willing or able to tell the higher-level and top-level leaders that they are failing to abide by the standards or principles of leadership that they claim to expect from others in the company—particularly those who are lower on the org chart than they are.

Leadership development/training is bound to fail (or at least not be as successful) if there is not support from the highest levels. This means that the highest levels first— and all levels in the company—must practice leadership in the desired way. As a senior leader, have an honest conversation with yourself and your team about this. Ask yourselves if you are really leading the way you expect everyone else to.

MICROMANAGEMENT

This is my favorite form of politics to talk about. Everyone loves to say how bad micromanagement is, how much they hate being micromanaged, and how evil micromanagers are. But no one ever stops to ask: where does micromanagement really come from?

Really, it's about fear. People generally don't want to micromanage others. If a manager is doing it, it usually means he or she is concerned about looking bad to someone. If the manager's boss or someone else who has power is threatening the manager for some reason (often political, to make that person look better or not look as bad), that's likely the cause.

Or it could be that the manager is one of the people who is trying to make someone else look bad and is therefore concerned that any mistakes his or her team makes would reflect badly on him or her and sabotage the path forward to a promotion, expanded role, more money, influence, or power.

Remember that a person's behavior (especially at work) is typically much more dependent on the environment than on the individual characteristics of the person. In the chapter "Scapegoating," we will delve more into the mistake related to this that people and companies often make, which is called the "Fundamental Attribution

Error." Until then, recognize and focus on the fact that most people don't go to work each day with the goal of being a micromanager. With very few exceptions, most people just want to do a good job every day—and that does not involve micromanagement. Yet we often put the blame solely on the person without looking at the situation that person is in. But the reality, as Chip and Dan Heath say in *Switch*, is that "what looks like a people problem is often a situation problem."

With all the negative talk about micromanagement, it is important to remember that, like cholesterol, micromanagement isn't always bad. If there are clear standards that someone is not meeting, then it could be legitimate as a way to coach and guide. Or if someone is new, then it's actually good to micromanage until the new hire demonstrates proficiency. In that case, people often don't micromanage enough, which is a whole different story. For more on that, look to Ken Blanchard's Situational Leadership model.

The Situational Leadership model says that managers should match the level of direction they give to an employee doing a task with the person's level of competence and confidence at doing the task. For someone who is not competent or confident, managers must use more of what the model refers to as "directive behavior," which is telling and showing the person clearly and specifically what to do. As the employee becomes more competent and confident with the task, the manager should reduce the amount of directive behavior and switch to more "supportive behavior," which involves less telling and showing and more questioning and providing feedback.

People can feel micromanaged when they are competent and confident yet the manager is still using a lot of directive behavior (and not supportive behavior). But when someone is new, if a manager uses too much supportive behavior and not enough directive behavior, then the person will often struggle to produce desired results and, ironically, may also feel "unsupported."

Apart from the Situational Leadership angle, however, the "bad" kind of micromanagement is often a symptom of politics inside the organization. You have to figure out what those politics are and then correct that political situation. The best way to solve micromanaging is to understand what are the situational barriers or fears that are causing the manager to micromanage.

If there are clear standards that employees are not meeting—or if employees are new—then it's fine to let managers "micromanage." But they should be able to articulate specifically how they are judging the employees' work to be complete, accurate, up-to-standard, and so on, as well as the plan for backing off once each employee consistently meets the standard.

Whatever you do to address it, remember that the way to root out bad micromanagement is definitely not to provide "anti-micromanagement training." Nor is it necessarily to fire managers—even if they seem to deserve it.

TREATING POLITICS

There is no such thing as the "only way" to treat politics. But most issues can be dealt with effectively using the framework and guidelines below.

TAKE OWNERSHIP

First and foremost, if the organization you run has become overly political or bureaucratic, own it. Be bold, admit it, and work with people to change it.

Yes, it's possible that you could be fired, sanctioned, or disrespected for admitting weakness or that it happened under your watch. But probably not. It's more likely that you will be praised for your courage, candor, and willingness to fix a bad situation.

A great example of this is on Gordon Ramsay's TV show *24 Hours to Hell and Back*, an exposé of restaurants that are failing and have absolutely horrifying food, service, and atmosphere. The restaurant calls in Ramsay and his team, who heroically transform it into something amazing—and in only twenty-four hours.

In almost every case, the owner of the restaurant is at the root of the poor performance. After Ramsay appears, the owner magically transforms into a great manager and immediately erases what is typically years of bad behavior.

Although this show certainly has a "formula" that is likely very staged, it is based in reality. Owners who acknowledge their issues and work to resolve them through open communication really do change. And the people who work with them genuinely appreciate it and are willing to move forward with them.

DON'T WORRY ABOUT THE CONSEQUENCES TO YOU

Let's think about the worst-case scenario for you if dealing with politics goes badly. Even if you get fired and publicly called out for being an idiot who never should run a company again, you still will recover—and probably even come out ahead. Everyone makes mistakes, including C-suite executives, company founders, and other high-level professionals.

Even Bill Belichick, arguably the greatest NFL coach of all time, got fired by the Cleveland Browns in 1995.

I'm sure you've had many transitions and made many mistakes in your career. The important thing is to learn from them and not to dwell on them. I've worked with and heard of countless people who have had career transitions, including the highest-level C-suite executives, and almost all of them end up getting something better than what they had when they were fired. Some have even said getting fired is the best thing that ever happened to them. So don't worry about getting fired or disgraced. Be brave and do the right thing.

HEAL PEOPLES' EMOTIONS

Another key point when treating politics is that you have to address and heal peoples' emotions in order to regain their trust, foster trust throughout the organization, and eliminate politics.

This theme parallels FBI negotiator Chris Voss's book *Never Split the Difference*. In it, Voss argues (correctly) that the reason people do poorly in negotiations is that they focus too much on the rational and logical brain. But negotiations, he says, are all about emotion—and messy emotion, specifically. After all, he says, it's hard to negotiate rationally with a crazed, heavily armed robber.

Same thing with office politics.

Too many people approach politics from a rational angle. They avoid dealing with the emotions because that's hard and painful—and they often think it's unnecessary, since emotions are not owned by the company but only by individuals. But, of course, that's ridiculous.

Like it or not, your company is made up of people who have emotions. You are one of the people in your company who has emotions. You should treat the company politics as you would a problematic marriage that needs to be saved. In marriage, if you are having problems with your spouse, you go to counseling and see a therapist.

Certainly, not every couple that goes to marriage counseling stays together. But many do—especially when both parties are open about the parts of the problems they own and are willing to work at it.

If the words "counseling" or "therapist" scare you, don't worry. You don't have to call it that. You can hire "executive coaches" or "organizational coaches" for yourself and for the different parts of the company.

Those coaches, who are often licensed therapists, can help you and your team craft and execute a plan to heal your own emotions and those of the people in the company. Just know that change and emotional healing are not going to happen overnight. Likely it will involve the coaches talking and listening to various people separately and then together in order to investigate what's going on from everyone's unique perspective, then working together toward a solution.

A truly neutral third-party person or group of people is critical for this process. Otherwise employees will not be truthful. And you and the coaches need to be crystal clear about your intentions of exposing and fixing the politics, so that everyone will be honest and reveal the whole truth.

Assure people that no one will be punished for speaking truthfully—even if not everyone agrees with their perspective. Label their emotions as precisely as possible when you're doing this. Tell them directly that you know they may be afraid something bad will happen. Promise it won't, and keep that promise.

You also have to assure people that you know the politics are not their fault and no one is going to be punished for having acted in a political manner before—as long as they own it and genuinely want to solve it and move forward. Acknowledging your role in the situation definitely helps here.

Tempting as it may be to have HR run the investigation

(since they are already in-house and often do this type of work), do not do this. Everyone knows that HR is never really neutral, and people will be spooked into thinking you're out to get them.

Since HR is part of the company already, they are too close to the situation to resolve it. But they should definitely speak to the external coaches, as they will likely be able to provide helpful context and detail.

DEAL WITH THE POLITICAL SITUATION

Let's look at three other situations that may cause politics in your organization but are not the fault of or associated with any one person.

Environmental issues often cause politics even if the people don't necessarily want to be political. They almost always need to be solved before politics can truly be cured.

We won't spend a lot of time here on these issues because they are actually critical flaws themselves, with dedicated chapters in this book. They are: Unclear Goals, No SOPs, and Dysfunctional Infrastructure.

If you have politics in your company that are dragging it down, first examine your goals. The first step of that is ensuring that everyone is completely aligned on how to evaluate success or failure in your company and in your company's goals. If they aren't, fix that and get everyone aligned.

Then, make sure each goal has a clear standard of success and that each goal is shared across the company. Again, if that doesn't exist or is not following the guidelines described in the chapter on Unclear Goals, address that. And if there are any goals that only exist for certain silos, get rid of those.

After you look at the goal issue, then examine your SOPs. Do you even have them? If not, then you need them.

If you do have them, are they up to the standards described in the No SOPs chapter of this book? If not, address that issue. Having clear SOPs is very helpful for cutting down on bad micromanagement, which cuts down on politics.

Finally, the third area is your organizational infrastructure. If the politics are too deeply rooted, the last resort may be that you need to redesign the organization to eliminate the politics. There's much more on this in the chapter on Dysfunctional Infrastructure. For now, suffice it to say that redesigning the organization to eliminate politics does NOT mean reductions in force or layoffs.

KEY TAKEAWAYS FROM THIS CHAPTER

- There are many different kinds of politics.

- Don't pretend that politics will go away if you ignore them. You must deal with them.

- Treat politics like a bad marriage and go to "counseling."

- Clear processes, standards, and goals, as well as a well-designed organization, are also necessary for eliminating politics.

BLIND SPOTS

Have you ever heard of the Johari window?

The Johari window is a psychological model that helps people see their blind spots: things that are known to others but not known to themselves. Just as people have blind spots when it comes to recognizing areas where they have an opportunity to improve, companies also have blind spots that hold back their performance.

A blind spot in the corporate setting is something that is happening or not happening that no one is aware of. Or it could be something that some people may be somewhat aware of but is hard to put into words. It can also be something that some people are somewhat aware of but no one knows how to deal with it, or wants to.

Companies often talk about wanting scalable and sustainable growth. They try to do things that create that.

How many times have you said to someone in your company, "That's a neat idea, but how can we scale it? Is it sustainable?" Too many to count, right?

But how often do you ask, "Why *can't we* scale that idea if it's good?"

Leaders are often blind when it comes to the critical flaws in their companies that prevent scaling. Often, it's not the idea that's unscalable; it's that the organization is unwilling or unable to adapt to make it scale. In reality, companies that have blind spots tend to *prevent* growth and peak performance in a scalable and sustainable way.

Below are three common and dangerous types of blind spots.

1. **Customer-focused blind spots.** This means being blind to the flaws in your products, services, or processes from the customer's perspective. It also means accepting the status quo and being blind to what it causes your customers to do—for example, leave you, avoid you, work around you, or fight you. Another form of this is being aware of the flaws but choosing to prioritize focusing "strategically" on something else.

2. **Internal politics blind spots.** Building on the previous chapter in this book, if you are not aware of your

company's internal politics, determine how they exist and what they are.

3. **Process blind spots.** This means spending time and resources on unnecessary processes that seem to add value but don't. This has some crossover with the Fixing the Unfixable flaw described in this book, but it's also worthy of its own discussion.

In the hotel industry, a tremendous amount of time is spent developing a budget for the calendar year for a particular hotel. Hoteliers call it "budget season" because it starts in about September and can last through mid-December. Sometimes even longer. (Side note: this issue is very common across many industries.)

The staff at the hotel spend tons of hours figuring out how much revenue and profit they think they will achieve in the next calendar year. Then, they have to present their budget over multiple rounds to senior leaders and other high-level stakeholders.

These budget presentations take hours and days to prepare for the top team. They also take days for the senior leaders who are stuck in all-day meetings listening to budget presentations. During the meetings the senior leaders challenge the hotel staff to defend their budgets. There can be some productive dialogue about strategy.

But usually it's a push-pull scenario. The senior leaders say the hotel should be able to do more. The hotel says doing more is impossible. They banter, using whatever statistics they can find to bolster their arguments.

Given the dynamic of the meeting, usually the hotels end up having to budget whatever the senior leaders say they have to budget. For example, 5 percent revenue growth and 6 percent profit margin growth vs. last year. Hotel teams become cynical about this because they know that even if they put together a solid argument for why the desired growth is unlikely, the senior leaders will overrule them and "shove a number down their throats" anyway.

If that's what's going to happen, there really should be no need for the budget process at all. The senior leaders should just tell the hotels the desired number. As long as the hotels don't have an objection, then there's no need for discussion.

Even if the hotels have an objection, there shouldn't be a need for an in-person meeting with a large group of people that lasts several hours. At the end of the day, this discussion is not about how value can be created for customers (which is always worth a detailed discussion). There's almost never any substantive discussion of how to improve real issues at the hotels.

Generally, this process is little more than haggling over

a simple goal or benchmark that the hotel will be evaluated on regardless of whether it is achievable or not. Even though almost everyone involved in the budget process hates the process, it still continues to happen.

And the process is expensive. Between time spent in meetings and preparing for meetings, as well as travel costs, a hotel company could conservatively save more than $6,700 per hotel by eliminating this process and allocating that money somewhere else. In a company that has ten hotels, that's $67,000, which is a lot of money.

BLIND SPOT SYMPTOMS

Depending on the blind spot, a lot of different possible symptoms can present themselves. In fact, many symptoms may be visible at once.

Frustrated and complaining customers and employees are often clear symptoms of blind spots. When a company does not meet its customers' needs—or when the company processes force customers to jump through annoying hoops, even if those hoops seem to be "necessary" based on existing conditions (which they probably really aren't if the company put some thought and effort into it)—customers get frustrated and complain.

When they complain, that frustrates employees, who generally hate dealing with frustrated or angry customers, even if that's in their job description. Employees particularly hate handling customer complaints when they know that there is a lot of bureaucracy in the company, for whatever reason.

Worse than customer complaints, however, is when customers don't complain. Even though it's less overtly confrontational and may seem like not such a big deal, it's the quickest way to destroy the company's revenue and profit.

If a customer has a problem and doesn't complain, more than likely it's because the customer knows that your company doesn't really care and is not going to try earnestly to fix the problem and prevent it from happening again anyway. So the customer just takes the easiest path and looks elsewhere—probably to your company's closest competitor, especially if that competitor is better than your company.

The hotel industry again is a great example of this. There are many statistics related to guest service scores, as you can imagine. One of the items that's often tracked is some form of the question "Did you have a problem during your stay?" Then, the next question after that is, "Did you report the problem to someone when it happened?"

Certainly, some customers complain to the company because they reported a problem and it didn't get solved to their satisfaction, and lots of hotels focus on that, which is fine. But what's really astonishing and what hotel companies (as well as many companies in other industries) don't focus on—or even see—is the number of people who respond that they had a problem but didn't report it to anyone. In my experience, I've seen this number be as high as 40 percent of people who responded stating that they had a problem but didn't report it.

Possibly there are a few whose problems were so minor that it didn't affect their experience in a significant way. But likely most of those guests are people who were affected and just realized that no one in the company would really do anything. Those guests probably just went elsewhere next time, thus hurting the revenue and profit opportunity at the hotel.

Like it or not, with so much consumer choice, you often only have one shot to make a strong, problem-free impression on the customer. If you don't capitalize on it (because you have a blind spot in your company about this), then you will start to lose customers, revenue, profit, and even employees—who will look to work elsewhere, since they know what your company is like.

All of this is what you need to stop. Right now, think about how many customers may be leaving you without even telling you. Do you even track that?

TREATING CUSTOMER-FOCUSED BLIND SPOTS

There are five parts to the framework for treating customer-focused blind spots:

- Listen, recover, and reflect

- Ask, "What sucks?"

- Anticipate needs

- Create personalized surprise and delight

- Use details

This framework also works for employees. But we will start with customers.

Perhaps most importantly, this framework is the key to creating brilliant, disruptive innovation. If your company is having trouble figuring out how to innovate effectively, use this to get "unstuck."

LISTEN, RECOVER, AND REFLECT

First and foremost, in order to fix your blind spots, it's critical to listen. Listen to anyone who is complaining, no matter how painful or annoying it is to do so. Even if you don't agree with the complainers, recognize that they are likely being genuine and experiencing something bad.

There's a saying in public relations: "perception is reality." This means that what someone perceives to be the situation is in fact the real situation for them. In this case, people who are complaining perceive a problem.

Even if you don't agree that something actually is a problem, you must acknowledge their perception that it is. Then you can work to either fix the problem (which is probably best)—or, if it really isn't a problem, then work to change their perception.

Realize that often the complainers will give you the keys to the kingdom if you let them. You let them by listening carefully to them and then working to figure out how to win them back.

In his book *Setting the Table*, Danny Meyer talks about creating a "great last chapter" for people when service has failed and you need to recover. By listening to the complainers in an intentional way, you can become aware of blind spots. Then, look to write a great last chapter not only by doing something unexpected and amazing to get them back, but also by figuring out how to prevent that problem from happening again and how to fix it quickly and effectively if it does happen again.

One important point on listening to customers: you listen to what their problems are in order to discover your blind spots. But you don't necessarily want to ask them for solutions, for what would make them happy, or for ideas on how to make the problem go away. That is for you to solve.

Plus, if you ask customers for solutions, you will often get ideas that aren't the best. After all, as Henry Ford (supposedly) said, "If I had asked people what they wanted, they would have said faster horses." Steve Jobs agreed: "A lot of times people don't know what they want until you show it to them."

Again, it's your job to listen to the complainers. But you and your team can often come up with better solutions than what customers would tell you—by thinking together and creatively about a great way to eliminate the problem forever.

Along these lines, in addition to listening to customers, do some self-reflection. Self-reflection can and should be for yourself, but it's also critical to do it at all levels of the organization in an intentional way. Have meetings designed specifically for this purpose.

Speak directly to everyone in the company—either in small groups or one-on-one, which are better for gathering this information than large groups. When you speak directly to people individually or in small groups, you get great, highly detailed, and relevant information. Chip and Dan Heath, in their book *Decisive*, call this "zooming in."

Raise your hand if your biggest fear is that your industry will be completely disrupted. Or perhaps you're reading this because your industry or company is already being disrupted. Regardless, that's OK. Here's your chance to really learn something meaningful from that and potentially leapfrog the disruption.

ASK, "WHAT SUCKS?"

In your meetings about this topic and for yourself as a senior leader as well, ask this simple (but tough) question: "What is it that we do that sucks?" Once you list all the answers for what you do that sucks (according to your customers—and your employees), then you need to do all you can to fix those things. This is often called "removing friction," a great phrase.

1-Click Disruption

My favorite example of removing friction is Amazon's "Buy now with 1-click" button. If only everything could be that easy. This is one of the most brilliant things a company has ever done to remove friction from what previously was (and in many cases still is) a very tedious, time-consuming, and frustrating process that many customers hate and which, therefore, prevents peak performance and causes customers to leave—or, worse, causes your entire industry to be disrupted!

Removing friction is one of the great ways to spark innovation, become a disruptor, or maneuver around a disruption.

Bobby's Training

Leading a training organization for a major global company, Bobby saw that the customers who were taking the organization's training hated it because it was way too long; it was disconnected from the real process that trainees needed to do; and there was too much irrelevant information. In total, the trainees were expected to do forty-five hours of online training to learn a process that would take them no more than thirty minutes per week to execute.

When Bobby was trying to figure out initiatives to tackle

for the year, he looked at this training because he knew it was something that everyone hated doing, and it didn't accomplish what it needed to accomplish. And yet...it was mandatory.

Not because of any law; just because it always had been, and many people honestly thought it was necessary and beneficial, even though it was not.

Bobby decided to flip the script. He thought: what would be an amount of time to train the customers on the process such that they would not hate having to do it and go to great lengths to just get the training done without actually paying much attention or learning anything? The process was complex enough that it was not something that could be learned in ten minutes or an hour. Bobby decided eight hours (one day) was a good amount of time—as in, "give me a day, and I'll give you what you need."

Once he decided on the amount of time that would be appealing to customers, he then planned how to overhaul the training to be effective in that amount of time. At first, he ran into a lot of resistance from people who didn't think it could be done. But once he showed that the existing training wasn't achieving the results it needed to, he got buy-in from key stakeholders and secured significant funding to move forward.

As a result of Bobby's efforts, along with the team that helped him, the training time was reduced from forty-five hours to eight. People appreciated the course because of its relevance. And they executed the process better in their roles, which led to greater revenue growth sooner than had previously happened—all while saving training costs.

The iPhone Revolution

In Walter Isaacson's biography of Steve Jobs, Isaacson describes how problem identification and correction was the approach that Steve Jobs took with Apple in order to create the "insanely great," life-changing products that Apple created.

The iPhone was a direct result of this approach. Apple (led by Jobs at the time) made the decision to prioritize developing the iPhone because they saw that the existing "smartphones" in the market were terrible. Consumers hated them, and Jobs knew Apple could do better.

And you obviously know what happened because you probably have an iPhone that you can't live without. Or if not, then whatever smartphone you have was heavily influenced by the iPhone.

The iPhone is a great example of a revolution that came from a minor but very effective variation of a blind spot treatment question. The question that led to the iPhone was, "What are our competitors doing that really sucks and that we could do better?"

The really cool part about removing friction and fixing what you or your competitors do that sucks and that your customers (or consumers in general) hate is that it automatically gives you a great company goal for the year (or quarter or month). And really...what's more important than fixing something you or others do that everyone hates? Certainly not some shiny new object, right?

Another variation on this approach comes from a question that you've probably asked many times. In this approach, you flip the script on that question and ask not "What can we do to scale better in a sustainable way?" but, rather, "What are we doing that's preventing us from being able to scale sustainably, and what should we do to fix that?"

When you ask the flipped question about what's preventing you from scaling sustainably, you also start to open your eyes to your blind spots and unlock the door to peak performance. Then, make sure you open the door and walk through it.

ANTICIPATE NEEDS

While we are on the subject of customers, let me talk

about customer service and how to fix that. This part of the framework is also a key to proactively delighting your customers before they have problems, which is a big part of treating customer-focused blind spots. For me, the foundation for this part of the framework started at a luxury hotel in Boston about twenty-five years ago.

Luxury Service

When I was a sophomore in college, majoring in public relations, I secured an internship at a very luxurious hotel in Boston. My internship was unpaid, but I was happy to have one and learn—until I found out that I had to go to new hire orientation. Even though I was an unpaid intern, I had to go, my bosses said.

They told me it would be four hours long—a full morning—on a Wednesday. "Ugh," I thought. "How boring." But I didn't have a choice.

The Wednesday morning finally came, and I got on the train from my apartment to go to the hotel. Then I thought, "Uh oh. I don't have anything to write with. If it's a four-hour meeting, I probably will need to write some stuff down, and I should have brought something to write with. Too late now. I hope I don't get in trouble."

My next thought was, "I'm kind of hungry. I don't know if

I'm going to make it through the class without food. That could really suck." Then, once again, "Oh, well. Nothing I can do about it now. I guess I'm stuck."

When I got to the hotel, the orientation was in the hotel ballroom. A beautiful ballroom. Hotel-branded notepads and pens were at every seat. I was relieved.

Then I noticed a table of delicious-looking pastries in the corner. Again...relieved.

Shortly after orientation began, Willy, the executive assistant manager (the second-highest person in the hotel) came in to give a lecture on service. I thought, "OK. Whatever."

He began by asking the class a question: "What do you think makes great service?"

"Product knowledge," someone said.

"OK," Willy responded. "What else?"

"Being friendly," another person said.

"OK. Anything else?" Willy asked.

No one else said anything. At that point, I wouldn't have

been able to say anything else even if they had paid me. After a short silence, Willy continued, "If you know your product and you are friendly, you can give good service. But what is it that makes great service?"

Silence. We were all stumped. Finally, after a long pause, he told us.

"The key to providing great service," he said, "is anticipation. Anticipating the customers' needs sometimes even before they do."

At that moment, for me, it clicked. I felt like I had just been struck by lightning. I flashed back to my concerns on the train that morning.

"Oh my God!" I thought. "I was worried about not bringing something to write with. But they provided pens and paper. I was worried about not being able to eat. They provided food. They anticipated my needs before I even knew what they were!"

Those things may seem trivial now, but they weren't then. And they actually aren't now either.

In that one instant, my life was forever changed. I understood completely, and it was hardwired into my brain. That lesson is something I will never forget, and it literally launched my career in the hospitality industry. Because I thought to myself, "That was amazing. Willy is amazing. I want to go to graduate school to learn to be like him."

Luxury Service—Twenty-Five Years Later

Fast forward the luxury hotel service story to twenty-five years later. I was attending a conference of the International Luxury Hotel Association (ILHA). One of the keynote speakers was Colin Cowie, one of the world's foremost luxury event planners.

He was presenting about how he provides great service at the events he plans. And the very first thing he talked about: anticipation. A timeless classic is a timeless classic for a reason.

Thinking about the pain your customers have provides you with the needs you can anticipate. Anticipating your customers' needs eases their pain and makes their lives better. Then you just have to provide one other thing: personalized surprise and delight.

CREATE PERSONALIZED SURPRISE AND DELIGHT

The best example of personalized surprise and delight that I've ever experienced was at a restaurant in New York called Eleven Madison Park (EMP), recognized today as one of the best restaurants in the world.

At that time, 2011, it wasn't yet there, but they were working on it, and it was already amazing on all levels. (It was owned at that time by Danny Meyer, whom I mentioned earlier as the author of *Setting the Table*.)

My wife and I were having lunch at EMP. It was a multicourse tasting menu of brilliant, delicious food. After the fifth course, a manager approached our table. "Did you go to Cornell?" he asked me.

How the hell did he know that? I looked around the room, stunned, wondering if someone I somehow knew was there. No one was.

After a pause, I decided I probably needed to answer. "Yes, I did," I said, incredulous as to why he would possibly be asking.

"Great!" he said. "We thought so. We were wondering if you would like to have your next course in the kitchen. We figured that with your background in hospitality you might be interested in seeing the kitchen and how we operate. If you don't want to, that's perfectly fine. But if you'd like to see it, we'd love to have you. We've prepared everything, and we're ready for you now."

I was blown away. I have always loved restaurants and fine dining. And I love seeing professional kitchens, especially great ones like this. I had never had service like this before.

When we got back to the kitchen, they introduced us to all the cooks and chefs, who were incredibly gracious. Then, they placed us at a special table overlooking the kitchen.

One of the cooks came over and prepared our next course right in front of us. It was delicious, of course. And so fun to watch.

We chatted in the kitchen for awhile, talking to everyone and thanking them profusely. The manager then escorted us back to our table where we finished our meal with smiles on our faces bigger than we'd ever had before at any restaurant. Absolutely extraordinary.

I asked the manager, "How did you know who I was?" (remember this was in 2011). He said, "We did a little research. We always like to do a little research on our guests to personalize the experience for them." Wow. Another revelation.

And yet, especially now, not hard to do. Today, all you have to do (and even then I'm sure all they did) is some easy research on the person or group of people on Google,

LinkedIn, or Facebook, and you can get what you need to help personalize the experience. There are a couple of other great, simple techniques as well.

That brings me to the final part of this section, which is how you can manage to consistently provide personalized surprise and delight: details.

USE DETAILS

That the staff at EMP knew where I went to graduate school is an example of a simple detail that helped them brilliantly personalize my experience. Here's another story from another area about simple details leading to personalized surprise and delight.

The Note

Brett, the leader at a company I worked for, had asked me to attend a meeting to facilitate a session for his team. I had to fly to the event and stay overnight for a few days. Not a big deal. Very typical. It was my job.

When I got into my hotel room, I found a nice basket with local packaged food and other goodies. And there was an envelope with a note inside.

The interesting detail about the envelope was that the

names on the cover were "Noelia and Rebecca," my wife and daughter, who weren't there. Even though Brett and I had a nice working relationship, I didn't recall ever telling him their names.

I read the note.

> Dear Noelia and Rebecca,
>
> Thank you so much for allowing Josh to be here at this meeting with me and my team. I know it is hard for you to be away from him, and I know he misses you a lot. But I want you to know that the work he's doing with me and my team is really important. He is helping us to truly be our best. And I am very grateful to both of you for supporting him being here with us.
>
> I hope you will enjoy the treats we put together for you as a token of our appreciation.
>
> Thank you again!
>
> —Brett

I got a little choked up. I immediately called my wife and daughter to tell them about this. We were amazed. We'd never experienced anything like that before. I will be forever loyal to Brett for that.

Notice that just by finding out a simple detail like the names of important people in my life, Brett created an incredible moment of personalized surprise and delight that will make me drop anything I'm doing if he calls.

Brett obviously asked someone I knew (probably his administrative assistant, whom I knew well) for my wife and daughter's names. It probably took him about a minute to get that information.

And we already know there is plenty of detailed information about most people available through the internet.

But there is another way you can get great detailed information about people very easily: just ask them.

Of course, you have to approach this a little carefully. You can't just say, "Hey, tell me the names of your wife and daughter so I can personalize your experience." That would kill the surprise and delight.

But there are plenty of ways to connect to people simply and easily in the course of natural conversation or interaction (whether that's in person, on the phone, via email—or even through a questionnaire or form). All you need to do, as you're forming the relationship with them, is be real and ask, out of genuine curiosity, about things they enjoy. Favorite food, movie, color, snack, drink, hobby.

If you do this right, it's easy to get a ton of information to help you personalize their surprise and delight.

Spaghetti and Meatballs

For example, I once helped organize and facilitate a meeting of high potential/high performing leaders in a company I worked with. As part of an icebreaker exercise, each member of the group was asked to name their favorite food. Even though they were all highly experienced, successful adult business leaders, amazingly more than half of them said their favorite food was spaghetti and meatballs.

So we decided one day to change the planned lunch menu to serve spaghetti and meatballs. All the attendees thought it was great. You should have seen the smiles in the room. Even better, it demonstrated the type of service the company wanted them to provide for its customers, which they were going to need to instill in their teams as future top executives.

The type of loyalty I have to EMP and to Brett as a leader, as well as the delight of the high potential/high performing leader group, is what you are striving for from your company's customers. You have the power to make it happen if you approach it correctly and use details.

It's not conceptually hard to do, but it does take effort.

The effort is worth it, though. And not just for surprising and delighting customers in a personalized way.

"I'm Sorry" Isn't Enough

Another key reason why you need details is because they prevent problems. In this case, I'm talking not about personalized details but about all the details associated with the customer's journey—or with a particular process, product, or service in your company.

We'll spend more time in the No SOPs chapter discussing the kind of process detail you need. But here, the important thing to remember is that the more detailed you are, the better.

Colin Cowie, the event planner I mentioned previously, frequently does events that can cost up to $25 million—just for the event. "At those prices," he said, "I can't afford to have a conversation that starts with 'I'm sorry.' So I have to go through every detail to make sure everything is perfect."

It may be tedious and challenging at first, but if you have good SOPs, it won't be that bad. It will actually be empowering for your employees (and for you and your executive team), because you will feel more in control, and you will have fewer blind spots.

TREATING INTERNAL POLITICS' BLIND SPOTS

We've spent a lot of time talking about customers and their complaints, what we or the competitors are doing that everyone hates, and how to anticipate customer needs and personalize their surprise and delight. Now let's refocus to treating blind spots related to internal politics.

The same framework we explored above for treating customer-focused blind spots still applies. All the treatments for politics apply as well. But there are two more tactics:

1. **Ask employees the following key question** (again, individually or in very small groups): "What do I not know that I need to know?" This is a great general question that will help you uncover unknown unknowns. And it's a pretty simple question that shows you are interested in listening to what the other person has to say—and that you want the truth, even if the truth is harsh.

    The good news with this question is that you can ask it anytime. If you make it a habit of asking this question regularly and informally, it will help prevent blind spots in your company.

2. **Implement an employee *disengagement* survey.** I

know this sounds crazy, but most employee engagement surveys are useless because they fail to focus properly on serious problems the company needs to fix but is unable to see.

Imagine if you went to the doctor for your annual physical and, instead of discussing the details of your specific problems, the doctor told you only that your health was a six out of ten? How would you feel about that? Even if your health was a nine out of ten, what if the one point you were missing would kill you?

If you go to the doctor for a pain in your abdomen, you don't just tell the doctor that you "mostly agree" with the statement, "I am in good health." If you did only that, your doctor would never be able to diagnose what is wrong with you and determine a proper treatment.

The premise of the annual physical and any other visit to the doctor is to expose symptoms and problems in detail so you can immediately diagnose and treat them before they cause further harm or kill you. And yet in the corporate world, employee engagement surveys almost never do this.

Because most surveys don't effectively ask about symptoms, leaders have a terrible time figuring out what's really wrong when scores are bad. In some cases, they simply ignore or dismiss and move on. In most cases, however, they spend tremendous resources and energy trying to find ways to understand the real problems. It's ridiculous, and everyone hates the process, especially if there is a lot of dysfunction in the organization.

Also, surveys that ignore symptoms mask unpopular reality. I've worked with many companies whose employees hated their jobs and whose organizations were highly ineffective, yet the employee engagement scores were strong. This happens a lot in highly political organizations when employees are afraid of "blowing the whistle" on the survey for fear of repercussions.

In order to truly cure internal politics and other employee-related blind spots, turn your employee engagement survey into an employee *disengagement* survey—a diagnostic tool that uncovers the details of what your employees don't like about your company. I'd recommend my Company Symptom Questionnaire (available on my website).

It may be painful the first time you get the results. But, unlike typical employee engagement surveys, there will be no mistaking what's really going on that you can't see. There will be no need to dance around the symptoms and problems—especially if you explain to employees ahead of time that you want their feedback; that you know there are issues in the organization that you can't see; that you intend to work with them to fix them; and that this survey is intended to help them be honest, so they don't feel the need to hide anything.

TREATING PROCESS BLIND SPOTS

As for processes that seem to add value but don't, all you have to do is stop doing those processes or change them to make them better. Believe me, most people will probably consider you a hero and thank you from the bottom of their hearts for doing that. It's often a quick win, too.

If you don't know which processes fall into this category at your company, think about it for a minute. You can probably come up with several rather quickly.

If not, ask your employees that specific question: "What are examples of processes we're currently doing that seem to add value but really don't?" This is also a great question to ask people that makes them feel heard and will probably help your employee engagement scores, too.

Then ask for ROI justification on those processes, like you

would for any other project or new initiative. If the ROI isn't there, kill or change the process.

If someone shows you that there is an ROI, be strongly critical, as there could be politics involved. If you or enough people have called the process out, there may not really be an ROI, and most likely someone is just trying not to look like an idiot for doing something that's been wasting company resources for a long time.

KEY TAKEAWAYS FROM THIS CHAPTER

- Listen to the complainers (perception is reality).

- Do solid self-reflection yourself and at all levels in the organization about what you and your competitors do that sucks and everyone hates.

- Prioritize removing friction, bureaucracy, politics, and worthless processes.

- Use anticipation and details to ease your customers' pain, make their lives better, personalize their experiences, and surprise and delight them. It will build lasting loyalty and grow your revenue.

- Write "great last chapters," like Danny Meyer, for any mistakes you make.

SCAPEGOATING

Did you know that eating less margarine prevents you from getting divorced?

According to a book by Tyler Vigen, between 2000 and 2009, there was a direct correlation between margarine consumption in the US and the divorce rate in Maine. Both of these things decreased dramatically during those years at very similar rates. So in order to ensure people stay married, we need to ban margarine everywhere, right?

It's pretty obvious that blaming margarine as a cause for divorce is insane. But it's a great example of a common form of scapegoating. And it's probably not that far off from what happens all the time in your company.

Scapegoating happens on the heels of blind spots. It's something that people inside an organization do sometimes out of ignorance and other times intentionally to deflect blame away from themselves when performance is not what it should be.

What makes scapegoating dangerous is that it's frequently effective in the short term for the people doing it. Authority stakeholders who want answers (investors, Wall Street analysts, the board) often buy into superficial excuses, so it's tempting to give them to get those people off your back. Sometimes it works. But probably not forever. If they catch on that you are just being superficial and scapegoating, they may turn on you at some point—and rightly so.

What complicates some forms of scapegoating (and helps make them effective for the people doing them but bad for the company) is that many times there is a correlation between what's being blamed and what's really going on, as we saw with divorce and margarine. However, correlation is not the same as causation. Other times, what's being blamed is some part of the problem even though it's not the totality of it, as the scapegoaters would have you believe.

One of the primary symptoms of scapegoating is that company performance does not improve after the scapegoated area has been addressed. For example, if the excuse for poor performance was that the wrong people were hired, and then the performance doesn't significantly improve shortly after a round of general and/or performance-based layoffs, implementing a new hiring process, and bringing in new people, then it's clear that wasn't the real problem.

In order to cure scapegoating, first diagnose how it typically manifests in your company. Then, dig deeper and look at all elements of the work environment in a systematic and thorough way.

Four scapegoats are commonly blamed:

1. **People**

2. **Obvious new things**

3. **Market conditions/the economy**

4. **Training**

Whenever you get told (or, more importantly, whenever you think) that one of these things is the root cause of your problems, be wary. And call bullshit as necessary.

PEOPLE

People are probably the most common scapegoat in

most companies when financial performance is down. Scapegoaters say things like, "The IT department is a bunch of lazy idiots," "We just don't have the right type of people to do the sales job properly," "We need better people," or "HR just isn't doing a good job hiring the right people" (note the brilliant double people scapegoat with this one—both the people being hired and the HR people are blamed).

Scapegoating people is kind of weird in a way because getting rid of people is one of the costliest things a company can do. There are so many costs and repercussions when you have to get rid of someone or a group of people. And there is so much hard, painful work involved in that process.

Think about all the costs ("hard" and "soft") associated with letting someone go. They're huge, right? And yet, so many times, companies incur huge costs and blame people for the company's problems when it's not their fault.

Companies wrongly blame people for a variety of reasons. Sometimes it's intentional and political, which is really bad. But mostly, it's a lack of understanding or ignorance.

Blaming the people when they aren't really the problem happens all the time in life outside of work, too. So it's bound to cross over.

Chip and Dan Heath, in *Switch*, argue that when it comes to lack of change (which is a form of poor performance by people), "What looks like a people problem is often a situation problem." This is what is known as the "Fundamental Attribution Error," where we attribute problems to intrinsic characteristics of someone's personality when really the issue is the environment.

My story revolves around my daughter and her homework. Although this comes from my personal life, I've seen countless corporate examples as well.

HOMEWORK

It began when my daughter first started getting homework in second grade. Every day when she came home from school, my wife would tell her, "It's time to do your homework." And she would say, "No."

They went back and forth and in a circle several times and almost always it ended in an argument. Inevitably, after the argument, my wife and I had discussions about what was "wrong" with our daughter. We would say things like, "she's lazy," or "she's stubborn," or "disobedient."

Look how easily the first thing we did was blame traits associated with her person and personality. And that's for our daughter—the one person we both love the most in this world. We would "punish" her by not allowing her to use her iPod before her homework was done, which, of course, led to more fighting.

After many fights, we realized that what looks like a people problem is often a situation problem. So we consciously shifted our discussions to think about how we could change the environment and the situation to make it work better.

We decided that our daughter needed to be in charge of when she did her homework, so we gave her ownership of that. We had her map out exactly when she was going to do it each day (subject to our approval and some necessary boundaries like it can't be ten minutes before bedtime). That worked for a couple of days.

But then when my wife would remind her, she started saying no again. So we figured that we needed to change the situation again and stop my wife from being the "reminder" or the "enforcer."

We made a deal: she could use her iPod to take a break after school and before starting her homework—as long as she did her homework without an issue. We programmed the iPod to give her an automatic reminder (ding-ding) at the scheduled time, so my wife wouldn't have to do it.

Like magic, my daughter immediately started doing her homework as soon as her iPod reminded her, without any discussion or fighting whatsoever. She wasn't lazy or disobedient. There was nothing wrong with her at all. In fact, she was great. She just needed a different situation.

Although this is a personal story, it is completely applicable to the business world. When you have someone who isn't doing something the way you want, figure out how to change the situation or environment to enable the proper performance. That's much more likely to be the cause than a flaw in the person's knowledge, skills, background, or "fit."

Geary Rummler, author of the seminal book, *Improving Performance: How to Manage the White Space on the Organizational Chart*, said my favorite quote about scapegoating people: "When you put good people up against a broken system, the broken system wins almost every time."

CHANGE MANAGEMENT

Speaking of the Fundamental Attribution Error and broken systems, let's talk about "change management," which is a huge fad these days, except that most corporate "change management" is bullshit. Not because the concept is bullshit, but because it is almost always structured around the bullshit assumption that whenever there is an organizational change, the people themselves need to be changed. This is wrong.

If you want people to change, change their situation and environment, which we will discuss below in the section on Treating Scapegoating. In *Switch*, the Heath brothers call this "Shaping the Path." It's important to understand that "we need change management," "we have bad change management," or "our people just don't like change" are just different forms of scapegoating people when the situation around a change is not dealt with properly in a company.

The other problem with typical corporate-style change management models is that they tend to focus almost exclusively on logic and rational items associated with the change, like mapping out stakeholders or creating a communications plan for each of the stakeholders to make them aware of the change.

Not that this is unnecessary. It's actually very important. And you certainly need a process for managing change in your company that includes things like this. But these things are more project management than change management. They aren't actually helping people to make the change that much, which is why changes in companies fail so often.

Obvious new things

These are things like technology or processes that people don't "want" to use or do. Obvious new things are often an easy scapegoat because it seems like everything was fine before the new thing came along—even if it wasn't.

Years ago, a major hotel company rolled out a new system for pricing its hotel rooms. This was revolutionary because, until that system came out, most hotels were setting their prices arbitrarily or based on a couple of data points. The system used a lot of good data to develop pricing recommendations, which is what made it more effective.

But the problem was that the people in the hotels did not always properly interact with the system to give it the inputs necessary for it to price correctly. Instead, they just "overrode" the system to price as they had always priced before.

When some hotels lost market share following the rollout, they quickly blamed the new system and said it was flawed and not working properly. This worked initially, because it was easy to comprehend and certainly a possibility.

But the implementation team for the system was eventually able to show that the issues with the system were users who weren't interacting with it properly. That was the real cause of the market share loss. But it took a while to show that, and there was a lot of debate, conflict, and lost time in between.

The lesson here is that it's important to consider all possible causes of poor performance even if there is one that seems so glaringly obvious that you are tempted not to look further (e.g., a new system that correlates with sudden poor performance). Although sometimes the obvious issue is the real root cause, often it is not—or, at least, it's not the only cause.

Dig deep and ask what other possible things could be causing the problem. Or delve into why the obvious problem could have begun.

Market conditions or "the economy"

This happens a lot in the restaurant industry. People say, "Oh, I opened the restaurant at a bad time." But really the issue is that the food, service, atmosphere, and price point were also bad. And the location was bad, too.

This happens in other industries as well, like the automotive industry. While it may be true that American car manufacturers are negatively affected by a poor economy, their poor performance is probably due more to

them having poor quality cars compared to foreign manufacturers from all perspectives—engineering, design,
branding, and pricing.

Oil and Gas Markets

A few years ago, there was a travel industry company
whose revenue had been down several quarters in a row.
The company as a whole was performing poorly, but in an
effort to explain away the poor performance as temporary
and not make the company management look guilty or
incompetent, several managers sought the highest con-
centration of poor performance.

It turned out that there were several markets with poor
performance in the company whose primary revenue-
producing industry was oil and gas (like certain areas
of Texas, Louisiana, and the Midwestern United States).
Since the oil and gas industry also was generally not doing
well at the time, the managers appropriated that explanation for why the overall company performance was down.

But the reality was much more complicated than that.
Underneath the surface, there were a number of other
reasons that contributed to poor performance, which
had nothing to do with oil and gas. The pricing and sales
strategies were suboptimal. Marketing dollars were being
spent on activities and media that had low ROI. Internal

customer service scores were very poor in several of the markets. And many more.

In this case, the oil and gas explanation was enough to placate the senior leaders and financial analysts who wanted answers at the time. But there was a lot left untouched that contributed much more directly to poor performance than just the decline of the oil and gas industry. As a result, the performance never really got much better.

Correlation vs. Causation

This is a great example of two things to be aware of. One is that there was significant value to be gained that was left untapped because the superficial explanation of "oil and gas" seemed good enough to prevent further exploration. Second is the difference between correlation and causation, which is often at the heart of scapegoating.

Certainly, there was a correlation between oil and gas markets being down and the travel company's performance being down. But it's a giant leap to say that oil and gas markets being down caused the company's poor performance.

Organizations leave a lot of value on the table and may actually wind up scaling poor performance by confusing correlation with causation, whether it's done intentionally or because of honest ignorance. It's really important to make sure you critically evaluate when someone gives you a causal explanation for poor performance. Generally, in order to prove causation, several things have to happen:

1. **The result has to happen every time the trigger happens and after the trigger happens.** In this case, it would mean that anytime an oil and gas market is down, company performance suffers. And company performance suffers only after the oil and gas markets are down. This should be true over multiple observations of performance or multiple time periods.

2. **The result should improve once the trigger goes away.** In this case, once oil and gas industry performance gets better, so should the company's performance. If not, then it's likely not the cause.

3. **All other variables that could trigger the poor performance must be ruled out.** In this case, as discussed, there were many other variables that were not examined.

So the next time someone gives you what they say is a causal explanation, consider these points and ensure they hold up before you accept the explanation as the true root cause. Remember, without a carefully designed, controlled experiment, it is very difficult to prove true causality. Be careful about making large, strategic decisions without doing proper research into true causality.

Although that experimental research can be expensive and time-consuming, it is generally much less expensive than going far down the wrong path because of a spurious correlation only to have to backtrack and change course. Although it may seem faster to make a quick decision based on a seemingly obvious, superficial, first explanation, it could actually slow things down considerably if the explanation is wrong or is missing some nuance.

Training

Training managers are frequently asked by senior leaders like you to conduct training for employees on a variety of general or specific topics (think: "negotiation," "influencing," "leadership," even how to operate a machine or software application) as a way to fix poor performance and poor processes (which are not training issues).

The exchange goes like this: you say to the training manager (usually while walking down the hallway after bumping into her and not in a formal meeting designed for needs analysis), "Hey...can you do a training on critical thinking and how to be both strategic and detail oriented for my team? They really need it."

And this is where the training manager has an opportunity to have a meaningful discussion that would stop this. But often, the training manager, in an effort to please you, her "client," will simply agree to do it. Then you work to set the wheels in motion.

This is like when people go into their doctor's office and ask for a particular medicine because they saw an ad for it on TV (or looked it up on the internet) and felt they needed it. In the doctor/patient situation, the doctor will not just say, "sure...no problem" without doing a thorough examination to ensure the medicine is really what the patient needs.

Instead, the doctor will ask for the symptoms that the patient is feeling that led them to believe they need the medicine. The doctor will combine the patient's explanation of the symptoms and medical history with his or her own knowledge and experience to make a diagnosis of the real problem or disease before deciding on a course of treatment.

This a dynamic that should be replicated whenever a training is requested. In the case of the doctor/patient relationship, the wrong medicine, in the worst case, could kill the patient. Best case, it just won't work, which will leave the patient frustrated and (over time) unsure of the doctor's competence.

In the business world, the same thing applies. Putting people through training they don't need in order to fix a problem that is caused by another variable besides training is not going to work. In the worst case, it will make financial performance worse or prolong poor performance and frustrate many people, which could have repercussions on a variety of things, including employee engagement and morale, as well as the top and bottom lines.

What makes the "training" scapegoat tricky is that training may play some part in the equation. It's possible that there is a lack of training or that the training is not good. And it's true that once the real issues are fixed, the training will need to be revisited and updated—and people will need to be retrained. But training is almost never the primary cause for poor financial performance—or even poor human performance.

TREATING SCAPEGOATING

In general, it's always best, whenever you have a performance problem in your company, to validate that there aren't issues in the situation or environment that are holding performance back. Few leaders do this because it's not the first thing they tend to think of, and it can be time-consuming and difficult to address environmental issues.

While it may seem tedious and overly structured to look at the environment first, do it. It's a total game changer. Remember my story about my daughter. And remember the Geary Rummler quote about people vs. a broken system.

Even if there are other scapegoat explanations (like the economy, training, or some obvious new thing), you still need to look at your internal environment. Since you will likely be (or perhaps already are) in panic mode when you are looking at your environment (because the numbers are bad and you need to fix them now!), it's best to have a systematic method for doing this, so you don't miss something, forget a step, or chase a shiny object.

My three-part method for ensuring you don't scapegoat is:

1. **Start with a needs analysis.**

2. **Uncover all root causes.**

3. **Change manage the emotional and the rational.**

START WITH A NEEDS ANALYSIS

Before proceeding with any kind of solution or treatment, ask for the perspectives of a number of people in the company and do a proper needs analysis. In particular, the training or organizational effectiveness team can be a great resource to lead this, since they often have a clear idea of what's really happening, as well as a background in conducting this type of discovery.

Rather than asking them for a specific training, ask instead for a thorough needs analysis. Tell them the symptoms you're having that you want to go away, and they should be able to take it from there—just like your doctor would. If not, call a consultant who specializes in this.

UNCOVER ALL ROOT CAUSES

This is definitely the most important thing to do to treat scapegoating, and it works hand-in-hand with the needs analysis.

There is a lot of literature on the subject of addressing the factors in your company's environment that contribute to poor performance. Some of these include the Behavioral Engineering Model from Thomas Gilbert; "Skill, Will, and Hill" from Seth Leibler; three levels of performance from Geary Rummler; and my favorite, the Exemplary Performance System (EPS) from Paul Elliott.

Basically, they all say similar things, so take a look at one or all of them and pick the one(s) that work best for you. Or work with your training or organizational effectiveness team—or a consultant.

Since there is so much detail associated with these concepts—and since several of these concepts are discussed later in this book—I won't go deep here. Below are the main environmental root causes of poor performance by people (and therefore companies) that you should always evaluate and consider as potential root causes and as part of the treatment plan.

- Lack of clearly established and shared goals and KPIs

- Lack of, unclear, or unaligned expectations about roles

- Lack of or unclear processes

- Lack of or unclear desired outputs

- Lack of or unclear standards of excellence ("sign-off tests")

- Lack of proper tools, reports, or information to make appropriate decisions

- Inappropriate reward structure, recognition, and consequences

- Inappropriate organizational design

Always look at the above root causes whenever there is a problem with company performance—whether it's financial performance (revenue, profit, market share, and so on) or human performance (that directly affects financial performance, of course). Recognize that what seems like the obvious answer someone has told you (or that you may be tempted to tell someone) may not be the real root cause. Also, it most likely isn't the only root cause—and it is never happening "in a vacuum."

Just like you must treat all the critical flaws in your company in order to turn performance around for good, you must also address all areas of the environment as part of the needs analysis and treatment plan if you hope to eliminate scapegoating.

Remember to review the criteria for true causality vs. mere correlation to help you with this. If you find there is only correlation and not true causation for what you think (or are being told) is the cause of your performance problem, dig deeper. Looking at all areas of the environment in a systematic way helps you do that.

CHANGE MANAGE THE EMOTIONAL AND THE RATIONAL

Finally, if you truly want to help people make a change, then not only do you have to make sure all the inputs to the environment have been addressed, thus "shaping the path," but, most importantly, you have to deal with their emotions (as Chris Voss says in *Never Split the Difference*).

By focusing your change management efforts on dealing with peoples' emotions about the change, as well as shaping the work environment (not just the people) to enable the change, then the change will take care of itself and be much more successful with a lot less pain.

One of the best ways to change manage the emotional realm is to talk through all the concerns people have about the change and all the things that are standing in the way of them making that change. Recognize there is fear underneath all of this, so you need to deeply understand those peoples' fears.

It's a great idea to ask them directly, "What fears do you have about this change?" Or "What exactly is making you hesitant or unconvinced about the change?" Then, listen to what they have to say and make sure you address it.

If you don't ask people directly, you will get helpful clues about peoples' fears from the resistance they provide.

Remember Bobby, the training leader from the Blind Spots chapter? When he initially presented his idea for reducing training from forty-five hours to eight, he described it as though he had "walked into a buzz saw." Everyone on the team he presented to yelled at him, told him he was crazy and said that it could never be done.

They went on and on about how the existing training was so thorough and comprehensive that people learned everything they needed from it. They talked about how it had always been in place and that there was no way people could learn all they needed to in such a short time. The resistance was so strong that Bobby had to stop his presentation and go "back to the drawing board."

But then, since he better understood their fears, he was able to re-present his ideas to the team in a way that proactively addressed their fears first through personal connection and emotion.

In his new presentation, the first slide was a picture of a fire hose next to a picture of a drinking fountain. The headline read, "If you're thirsty, which of these would better meet your needs?" Then, at the bottom, he wrote, "Sometimes more isn't always better. Sometimes you need just the right amount at just the right time."

Immediately the team he was trying to convince understood on an emotional level. They all laughed and shook their heads.

Then, on the next slide, he showed the team a picture of a woman staring at a computer in frustration. He asked them, "What emotions is this woman feeling right now?" Immediately, everyone started laughing and shouting their answers: "angry," "frustrated," "annoyed," "overwhelmed," "bored," "numb."

"Great descriptions," Bobby encouraged them. "How many of you have ever felt like that whenever you have taken a training—or one of our trainings?"

Smiles and nods all around.

"And when you felt that way, how much did you really learn?"

They all shook their heads again—only this time more quietly and in complete agreement.

"Clearly, there is no way people are really 'learning' from the training we currently have," he concluded.

Right after that, they asked him what he wanted to do. He went through the rest of his presentation, which outlined his plans and the ROI (the "path" with all the logical stuff). He quickly got permission to move forward with a funding request and commitment from the team to support that request.

What's remarkable about this story is that even with a clear ROI on the project (which was unchanged since the "buzz saw" episode), he never would have gotten buy-in on the change without first managing the personal, emotional connection.

KEY TAKEAWAYS FROM THIS CHAPTER

- Consider causality vs. correlation before placing blame and treating. Otherwise, you could give the wrong treatment, which, like in medicine, is bad. There is a sliding scale from neutral/bad to really awful.

- Look to all inputs in the environment before blaming people or other scapegoats.

- In addition to having a dedicated change management process, focus on peoples' emotions and on "shaping the path" in the work environment to enable a change to take hold and succeed.

UNCLEAR GOALS

I like to cook, and I often use food-related metaphors. Whenever I think about the critical flaw of Unclear Goals, I think about onions.

When onions are raw or not treated properly, they stink and sting, and they make you cry. That's a reasonably accurate description of what it feels like to work in a company that has unclear goals.

Also, like an onion, the flaw of unclear goals has multiple layers that need to be peeled back to get to the root.

And just as onions form the basis of many soups, sauces, and other dishes, companies need clear goals as a basis for true success.

THE LAYERS OF UNCLEAR GOALS

There are three layers of unclear goals:

1. **Misaligned Key Performance Indicators (KPIs) and success metrics**—when the company has not aligned on what its KPIs are and how to determine whether the company is successful or not.

2. **Imprecise measurements**—when the goals themselves don't have a specific measurement or standard of acceptability, or when the goals keep changing as leaders chase shiny objects.

3. **Poor applicability**—when goals aren't shared across the company.

LAYER ONE—MISALIGNED KPIS AND SUCCESS METRICS

Years ago, at a major hotel company, the corporate front office department was placed on the organizational chart under the "commercial services" division. While this was certainly reasonable, since the front office delivered a number of commercial services (like upselling premium rooms), several other parts of the company also felt like they "owned" front office.

Different brands had different standards for front office,

which affected the department. The operations division that staffed and ran the individual hotels also believed they were in charge, since they were responsible for front office performance at each of the individual hotels.

The problem was that none of the various groups who thought they "owned" front office really paid attention to each other. Each group simply told the leaders of the corporate front office department what they expected, and the corporate front office leaders had to sort it all out for themselves and do the best they could.

While front office performance wasn't awful, it also wasn't perceived as great either. No one could really articulate why.

As this story shows, flaws in layer one often take the form of different parts of the organization having different ways of measuring success—with no central alignment on the KPIs. (A variation is having multiple success metrics that aren't clearly prioritized.)

Layer One Symptoms

One symptom of lack of alignment on success metrics is that employees do a lot of work that doesn't move the needle on performance. Sometimes this is just busywork that adds no value. But many times this symptom manifests itself as certain silos or people doing well, even though the overall organization is not.

For example, sales and marketing might say, "We're doing a great job because our metrics are great." But in spite of this, the company overall is still performing poorly.

Now, maybe that's because some other metrics—like operational metrics—aren't working well and that's holding things back. But more than likely it's that the sales and marketing metrics just aren't real drivers of company performance, and the lack of focus is what's causing the problem.

Another symptom stemming from this layer is disconnects or even infighting among different parts of the company working toward achieving different metrics that are occasionally in conflict with each other.

For example, hotel salespeople are often bonused solely on booking business. So as long as the salespeople book a certain volume of business, then they make their goals.

But there are many days when a hotel may not need business from a group that's booked by a salesperson. On days when there is a lot of demand, hotels are often hindered by a lot of business booked by the salespeople at low rates when there could have been much higher-rated business booked through other avenues.

On those high demand days, the hotels will lose market share and revenue compared to what they could have achieved if they hadn't been filled with low-rated group business. The people in charge of the hotel's revenue, who are accountable for market share, will be scolded for poor hotel performance. And they will complain—both to the sales team and to everyone else—that it's the sales team's fault for booking low-rated business when it wasn't necessary, which is technically true.

But even though the hotel overall will perform poorly, the salesperson who booked the business will be happy because she made her goal. Based on the conflicting metrics, that salesperson is not concerned that the hotel lost market share, because that doesn't affect her. She may not even know that the business she booked caused market share loss—or if she does know, then she doesn't really care because she's made her goal anyway.

A second example of conflicting metrics is often revenue vs. profit or unit growth vs. profitability. Companies do a lot of activities to drive both revenue and profit. But in some cases, while attracting certain customers may increase revenues, it will decrease profits.

Similarly, in other cases, a company could build more units or expand into more territories, and so on. But those additional units or territories may not have the same profit margins or revenue expectations as the existing ones.

Ultimately, companies should have clear guidelines around the overall most important (or highest priority) organizational metric(s). If they don't—and certain parts of the organization are measured only on one or the other—then this will hold back financial performance and cause unnecessary effort and conflict for the employees.

Layer Two—Imprecise Measurements

Flaws in layer two are all about goals that don't have a specific measurement or standard that indicates they've been met.

Everyone knows about creating SMART goals (Specific, Measurable, Achievable, Relevant, and Time-Bound). But it's surprising how many companies and their people don't always use them. Instead, they will have goals that are more conceptual in nature, like "Be the top choice for prospective patients needing healthcare" or "Scale the current process for fulfilling orders."

While at first glance these goals seem reasonable, they are

missing a key component that shows exactly how anyone can know whether the goal has been achieved or not. For example, what does "top choice" mean? How will you measure that the company is the "top choice?"

Chances are you may have something in mind—as in, the number one hospital according to *U.S. News & World Report* or something like that. If that's the case, then make sure you put that into the goal specifically. Otherwise, it's open to interpretation, and you should put some thought into how you will actually measure it before putting the decided measurement into the goal.

Using our example above, for "scale the current process," again, what exactly does that mean? How will you know whether it's happened or not? What's the standard?

Does it mean that upon achieving the goal, you will now be able to serve 1,000 more customers without adding extra labor costs? Or perhaps it means that you will now be able to use the same process outside of your primary country of operations? Another possibility could be that you can handle an additional 15,000 orders without increasing your error or failure rate.

Without knowing exactly what the standard is, it's hard for anyone to achieve a goal properly.

Usually, flaws in layer two happen because leaders just don't realize how precise they need to be when it comes to goals. It could also be because they don't know exactly what they need to do to truly advance the organization.

But sometimes leaders will intentionally leave goals vague in order to have some "flexibility"—in case they don't make it or things change. This allows them to introduce an element of subjectivity if their own performance is judged poorly. In that case, they can transfer some of that blame to the people below them and make it so those people don't make their goals.

Another situation that results in vague goals is when leaders know that what they have to achieve is going to be very hard or nearly impossible. In this situation, they keep the goal wording vague to ensure they and their people aren't committed to something impossible.

With vague goals, people in the company won't truly understand exactly what results they are accountable for. As a result, they won't work as hard to achieve them because they know how easily they may change. Vague wording also makes everyone insecure because they never know if what they are doing is going to be good enough.

I have worked with many companies where no one really

knew if they were going to get a bonus because the goals were never clearly defined. Lots of people would ask, but no one (except maybe for the C-suite executives) really knew. It's very demoralizing for an organization.

Regardless of peoples' feelings and thinking only about the financial performance of the company, how can people do proper work to truly advance the company if they don't know exactly what they and the company are trying to achieve?

If there is not a clearly defined and measured outcome for a goal, then whether or not a goal has been achieved can be a matter of debate or subjective interpretation. Employees who have been working toward the goal and doing a lot of work will feel like they deserve a reward (bonus, good performance review) for their work.

But if leadership does not believe the goal has been achieved due to a different interpretation, then this can cause problems. Employees can become frustrated. The business suffers because all the employees are putting forth effort and spending money, time, and other resources doing things that aren't going to achieve the goal as the leaders intended.

Not knowing the true specifics of a goal is like playing a sport without keeping score. At that point, it's just a game.

That's fine if there's no need to win and it's just practice. But that's not business.

The third layer in the critical flaw of unclear goals is not sharing goals across the organization. This can happen for any number of reasons.

It could be that goals were developed by individual functions without consulting a cross-functional team. Also, it's possible that individual team-developed goals were not approved by cross-functional leadership at the same time. Third, it could be that individual goals only appear for the individual teams without any official goals that come from other parts of the organization—for example, if a company-wide initiative is not on the marketing department's goals. Or if the marketing department's goal depends on working with the finance department but finance does not have a specific goal to be part of the marketing goal.

If a goal is not shared across functions, it is much harder to achieve—especially if the goal depends on different functions working together at some point in the process. Most significant goals involve collaboration among many different functions for a variety of reasons and at a variety of touch points.

If the goals aren't shared, one department that is critical to the goal's success may not want to participate or may put working on the goal at the bottom of their "to-do" list. Of course, this not only makes the goal more difficult to achieve, it also can cause conflict and animosity among departments.

Even for the department that's choosing not to engage, requests for collaboration can be annoying and distracting when they know their own goals have nothing to do with those collaboration requests. And if they finally give in to the collaboration requests, that could put their own goals in jeopardy of being achieved, which is unfair to them and unproductive for the business.

TREATING UNCLEAR GOALS

To cure the flaw of unclear goals, you need to make sure that:

- Everyone agrees on exactly how to evaluate success or failure

- Everyone agrees on what success looks like

- Each company goal has a clear standard for success

- Each goal is shared by everyone in the company

- There are no siloed or functional goals

You accomplish this by treating each layer of the flaw, in order.

LAYER ONE

Treating layer one first means that you need to make an effort to get everyone officially and formally aligned on overall KPIs, success metrics, and what success looks like. Ideally this is done by bringing together all involved leaders (and even some lower-level implementers) and making a collective decision while everyone is in the same room—after getting input from everyone.

Although this may seem time-consuming and burdensome, it will save time in the long run with implementation and by helping to eliminate unanticipated delays due to different parts of the organization that are not aligned. Of course, if it's not possible to get everyone together for some reason (though I'd recommend you try hard to do it since it will be worth it), there are other ways. Let's go back to our corporate front office example.

One day, the training department and corporate front office leadership got together and realized they needed to do something differently. They realized that the reason why there was so much spinning and such mediocre results was that they didn't really know what success meant. It actually meant different things to different people.

To fix this, they interviewed key people via phone from all the stakeholder groups who thought they "owned" the front office. They asked them, "How do you measure whether front office is successful?" Based on the answers, they were able to identify three key metrics.

They then got all stakeholders together on a call to report the results, review the three metrics, and get everyone aligned and bought in. From there, they were able to refine their processes to drive those three key metrics. That never would have happened if they hadn't first created alignment on the success metrics.

LAYER TWO

Now that we've talked about what alignment on success metrics means, let's look at the second layer and discuss how to create clearly defined goal standards. "Clearly defined" means as specific and numeric as you can possibly be. For example, "introduce two products by May 1 that achieve at least 5 percent market share within the first three months of launch."

Let's break down the intentionality of this goal. First, we

have the numeric standard for the number of products. We're looking for two. Not one or 1.5. Two.

Then, we have the deadline by which they need to be introduced (May 1). We know from this that if we introduce two products on May 12, we have not met the goal. But there's more, of course.

Notice that it's not enough to just introduce them. They have to achieve at least 5 percent market share. Again, not 4 percent or 2 percent or 0 percent. Five percent or more. By adding this, we know that if we introduce three products that only achieve 1 percent market share, we have not met the goal.

Finally, there is the standard for the length of time when the market share can be achieved—within three months.

Put all this together and there should be very little that is up for debate about whether or not the goal has been met.

Also notice that we could have left out several components of the goal if those components did not matter. But in order to do that, we would need to have made a conscious choice (and gained alignment on that choice) to leave something out.

It's really important to translate concepts into numbers

in order to avoid having a goal that's not clearly defined. There's a simple exercise I do with leaders and teams that illustrates this very clearly. I'll do it with you right now. Feel free to use this with your team(s).

An Exercise in Clarity

Take out a piece of paper and write down the following four words, one underneath the other: "Always, Often, Sometimes, Never."

Now that you've done that, write down the percentage you associate with each word. For example, if you were to say, "I always brush my teeth with my left hand," what percentage of the time do you actually do that? You must pick one number as your percent (e.g., 63 percent). You cannot pick a range (e.g., 60-70 percent).

Now, write down the percentages you associate with each word. Then read on.

OK, now that you have your percentages next to the words, I will share mine below:

- Always: 100 percent

- Often: 70 percent

- Sometimes: 40 percent

- Never: 0 percent

Look at your percentages, and see how they compare to mine. Are they exactly the same for each word? I bet you they aren't.

Even if we agree on one or two percentages to be associated with a word, there is likely a lack of alignment around at least one. For example, I said "often" means 70 percent of the time to me. If you said any number other than 70 percent, then that's a lack of alignment.

What do you think of the misalignment between you and me based on this exercise? Interesting, isn't it?

Even words that seem to be concrete and clear (like "Always" and "Never") frequently have misalignment between two or more people. As an example, I've seen many people associate "Always" with 90 percent or 95 percent of the time. And I've seen many people associate "Never" with as much as 5 percent or 10 percent of the time.

I've even seen a couple of people who associate "Always" with 70 percent of the time! This fascinates me because, to me, that's nowhere near "Always." But to those people, it is.

Now, let's think about the impact this can have in the world of goal setting. If our goal is to "Always" satisfy customers (based on our agreed upon definition of "satisfy"), to me that means 100 percent of our customers must be satisfied, or we can't claim that we've achieved the goal. But the person who thinks "Always" means 95 percent, 90 percent, or 70 percent will think the goal has been achieved even if 5 percent, 10 percent, or 30 percent of our customers are not satisfied.

You can see the potential for conflict here. And that's without even delving into how we will measure whether a customer is "satisfied."

So what's the solution? Place a numerical value(s) in the goal itself. Instead of "Always" (as with this example), use a percent—whatever percent you want to use that you associate with "Always" (I'd use 100 percent, of course, but it's up to you). The percentage you use can be easy or hard to achieve, depending on the goal and what you're trying to do with your company.

Once you've decided on the number, show it to everyone involved in the process and gain alignment and buy-in. Be prepared for discussion and debate during this process—especially when you define not only the goals in numerical terms but also the words associated with them, like "satisfied," which you may define as something like "a rating of nine or ten on the first question of the customer service survey."

It may take a bit longer or a bit more thought to finalize your goals using this approach, but it will be worth it because everyone will be on the same page and will be crystal clear about what you're working toward, as well as what the boundaries are.

LAYER THREE

Once you have aligned on success metrics and established clearly defined goals for the company, make sure those goals are shared by everyone in the company. And I mean everyone. If there is anyone or any department that doesn't have the exact goal you agreed on, that's a problem.

Also, on the flip side, this means you need to eliminate siloed or functional goals that may be separate from the overall company goal. Those siloed goals are just a distraction that will prevent your company goals from being achieved.

It is okay to detail which functions, departments, or people are primarily responsible for certain parts of the goal. That's part of good planning and clarity of "swim lanes." It helps companies be more effective and efficient by eliminating confusion about who is supposed to do what.

But resist the temptation to bonus certain functions, departments, or people on only their parts of the goal. In order for this to truly work, everyone needs to have the exact same goals.

Doing this not only helps treat the Unclear Goals flaw. It also works to help treat the critical flaw of Doing Too Much and the critical flaw of Chasing Shiny Objects. Indirectly, it can help with cutting down on politics as well.

Just be careful about scapegoating if certain people do their part while others don't. Everyone needs to be on the same team and support each other.

The good news is that most people naturally want to do this—even if they sometimes have to provide some extra help to another function. They just need an environment that allows, encourages, and, in the best case, systematically forces them to support each other—and then rewards them for doing so.

Keep Score

In order to support each other properly, everyone needs to be able to see the score. Earlier in this chapter, we talked about the analogy that having goals that aren't clearly defined is like playing a sport without keeping score. This part of the treatment is a natural extension of that.

Once you have created clearly defined goals and shared them across the company, then you need to track them. The tracking needs to be visible to everyone. And the visibility needs to be clear and simple—as in, by looking at the tracking dashboard (or other mechanism), anyone (even a child that knows how to read) should be able to tell within thirty seconds whether the goal has been met or not—or the progress toward the goal.

For this, think about the thermometer graphics used with fundraising. For goals that have an element of time to them (e.g., Make ten sales calls per month), pace graphs are particularly helpful. Speedometer graphs can be great, too. There are lots of possibilities. (See below for some examples.)

BUDGET VS. ACTUAL

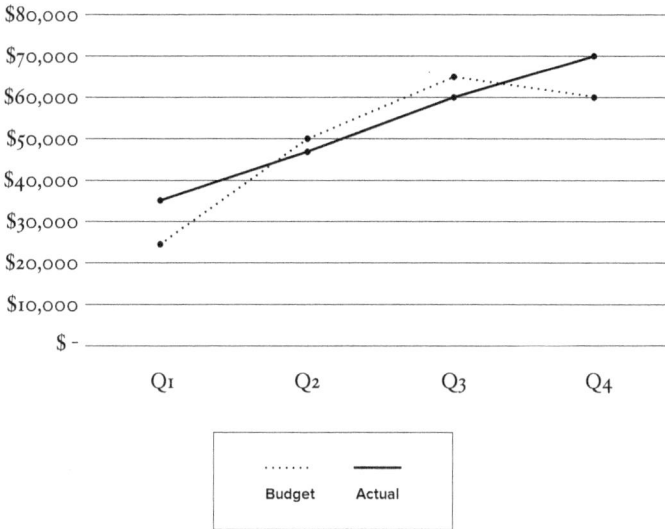

Legend:
Budget (dotted) · Actual (solid line)

$80,000
$70,000
$60,000
$50,000
$40,000
$30,000
$20,000
$10,000
$ -

Q1   Q2   Q3   Q4

Budget   Actual

ERROR BY MONTH

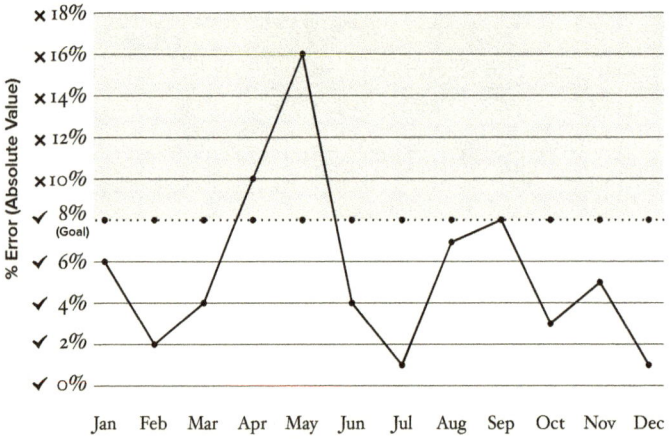

REVENUE COMPARISON

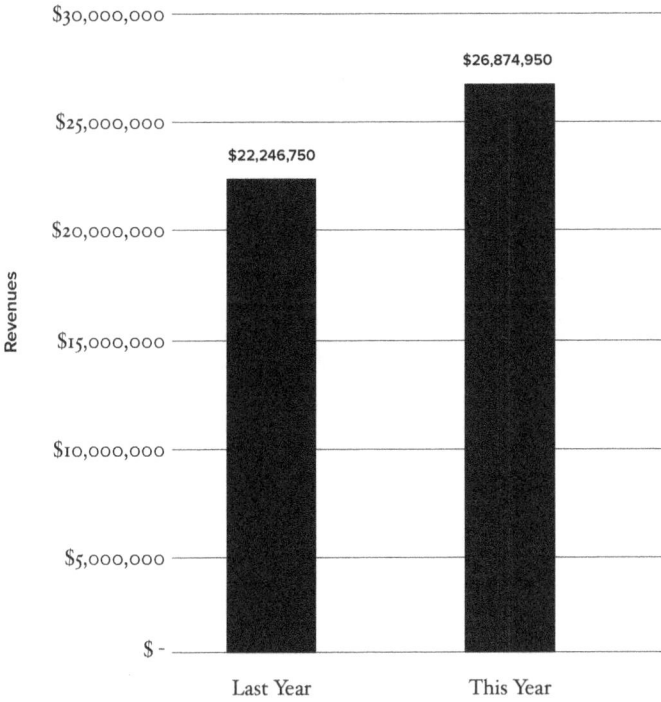

REVENUE VS. LAST YEAR

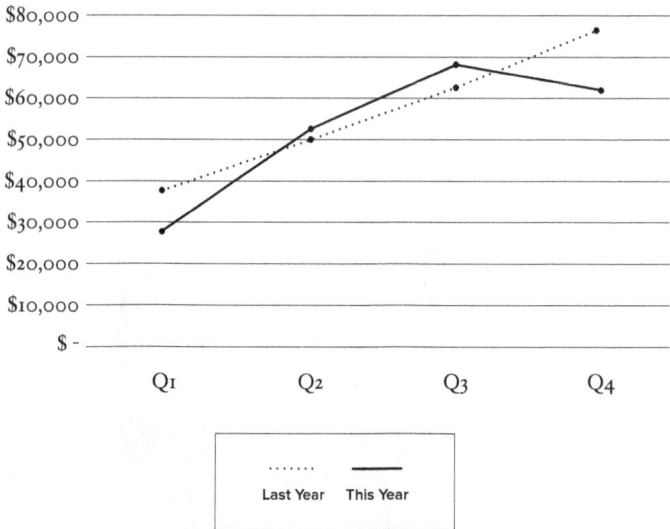

Last Year   This Year

YTD FORECAST ERROR

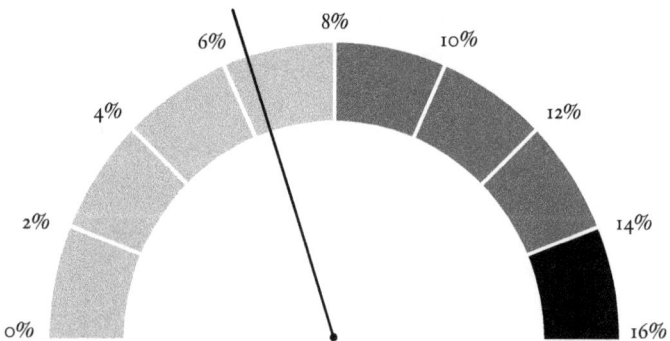

YTD REVENUE VS. BUDGET

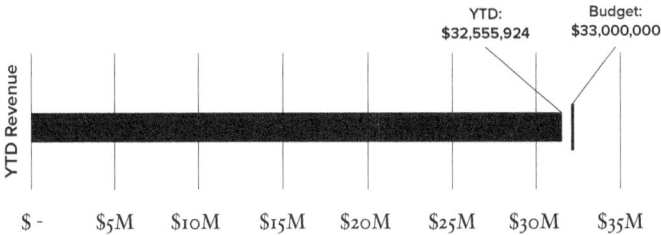

YTD:
$32,555,924

Budget:
$33,000,000

YTD Revenue

$ -　$5M　$10M　$15M　$20M　$25M　$30M　$35M

YTD REVENUE VS. LAST YEAR

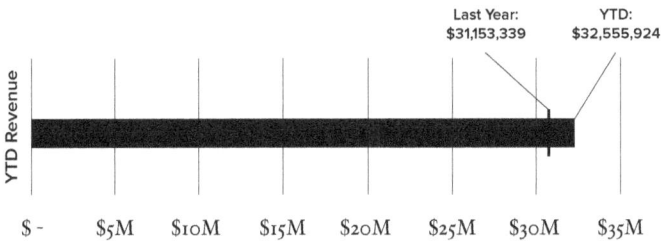

Last Year:
$31,153,339

YTD:
$32,555,924

YTD Revenue

$ -　$5M　$10M　$15M　$20M　$25M　$30M　$35M

The important thing here is to not only have simple, clear, visual tracking for the outcomes but also for the activities you plan to do to get to the outcomes. This is where a lot of organizations fail to be disciplined. Often they just track the outcome but not the activities. But it's critical to track the activities, because if you aren't achieving the activities, then you know why you're not achieving the outcome. On the other hand, if you are achieving the activities but still not the outcome, then that's a sign that you may be doing the wrong activities, and you should reevaluate the activities you're doing and potentially figure out new ones.

If you don't track activities, you'll never be able to properly diagnose why you're going off track. That could lead you down a fruitless path of chasing shiny objects, fixing the unfixable, or any number of other possibilities that won't really solve your problem.

Don't ignore the advice about keeping the tracking simple, clear, and visual. Remember that we're talking grade school simple as the standard.

Many companies have green, yellow, and red charts to indicate progress on a goal or project, which is fine. But if that's just part of a spreadsheet that has tons of details, then the quick assessment piece of whether you're achieving your goal or not is getting lost.

In another comparison, your visual tracking should be as simple as looking at the scoreboard for a baseball, basketball, football, soccer, or hockey game—or any other sport, for that matter. When you're watching a game and someone comes in from outside the room and asks, "What's the score?" anyone in the room can shout it out within ten seconds. That provides clarity and builds solidarity, both of which are critical for achieving goals.

KEY TAKEAWAYS FROM THIS CHAPTER

- Make sure everyone agrees on KPIs and how to evaluate success or failure, as well as what success looks like.

- Be as precise and numerical as possible when establishing goals.

- Make goals shared across the company for everyone and eliminate siloed goals.

DOING TOO MUCH

Have you ever been in a meeting or on a conference call and checked your email or phone because you were thinking about something else? Come on, of course you have. Everyone does it.

Now think...do you remember every detail about what was discussed in the meeting or on the call when you did that? Probably not, right?

How about this one...have you ever been asked a question on a conference call or in a meeting while you were "multitasking" and had to embarrassingly ask for the question to be repeated because you weren't paying attention? I bet that's happened to you before, too, hasn't it?

What the above examples show is that even you, a highly experienced executive, failed at doing even two simple things at once—checking your phone while listening to someone else. And yet, many companies set out to do huge numbers of initiatives each year to drive performance.

I have worked with companies that had more than fifty different goals across silos and functions—and that's just for one year!

If we as people can't even check our phone and listen to a conference call or meeting at the same time, how can we expect our entire company to do well on ten, twenty, thirty or more goals?

There has been a lot of research that shows that multitasking is not really beneficial or even possible. That, really, what people are doing when they "multitask" is just rapidly switching between multiple topics without putting proper effort or thought into any of them.

Think about your own daily situation, where you likely bounce from meeting to meeting about so many different topics that it's hard to even remember what they are, let alone all the details of them.

The results of multitasking are typically far worse than if someone focuses on one task exclusively, completes it, and then moves on to the next task.

The critical flaw of doing too much is the corporate

equivalent of a person poorly trying to multitask. Trying to complete tons of initiatives to drive performance in a given time frame doesn't really work and it causes lots of problems.

In order to really fix the performance in your company, stop doing too much. Stop trying to multitask and spread everyone too thin. Instead, focus everyone in the company on the "vital few."

WHY DO COMPANIES DO TOO MUCH?

Focusing your company on the vital few is hard. There are a lot of great possible initiatives out there at any given time and a lot of things you are accountable for achieving. It is very tempting to try to keep adding things to accomplish and wind up doing too much.

But to help break down this barrier, let's first examine why companies do it. Below are four common reasons.

- **The company is large and matrixed.** Doing too much often happens because the organization is so big that it seems impossible for all leaders and functions to get together and collectively decide priorities. Even if the executive leaders agree on certain general priorities, the trickle-down process tends to fall apart somewhere between upper management, middle management, and the performers who actually do the work.

Or sometimes the executive leaders are in on it because everyone knows that each part of the organization "needs to own" their respective part of a large initiative, since that department is already in existence. The people there need something to do this year.

- **You don't want to miss out or be left behind.** A second reason why organizations tend to do too many things at once is because the world changes so quickly that they feel like if they don't do a ton of stuff all the time, they won't keep up with the changes in the world.

- **Something to prove.** Sometimes companies wind up doing too much because senior leaders feel like they need to show how much they are able to accomplish in order to show their value as leaders to the key stakeholders, especially investors, the board, Wall Street, and so on.

- **Believing in the machine gun approach.** Some leaders feel like doing a lot is the key to innovation—as in, "Let's just do a whole bunch of things and see what sticks. If we do a lot, something innovative and great is bound to happen in some area." I call this the machine gun approach—just "spray and pray."

Unfortunately, the reality of this situation is that by doing so many things, organizations actually move slower. Think about all the time spent in meetings and calls figuring out what takes priority or when key people aren't available.

Then, there's also the issue of money and budgets. When a company decides to do ten or twenty things in a year across ten different functions, there is a lot more competition for budget. And likely companies are giving budget (and, even worse sometimes, time) to projects that aren't going to make a huge impact.

SYMPTOMS OF DOING TOO MUCH

Let's look at the symptoms of doing that, which most companies don't actively think about. There are a number of painful symptoms that appear in a company that's doing too much.

First and foremost, goals don't get accomplished. Or if they do, the result is half-assed—just enough to check the boxes so people can argue that they deserve a bonus or a good performance review but not enough to really make an impact on the company's performance.

Another one that I see often is duplicate work, where multiple departments wind up doing the same project when they don't even realize it.

In some cases, the work of one department will conflict with another. This can result in a culture of politics and frustration, as well as potentially wasting a lot of time getting approval from all parts of the matrix.

Doing too much also stretches resources and kills deadlines because, in an attempt to collaborate, everyone has to be on every committee, and then everyone's schedule gets bogged down in meetings or calls that are pointless or don't go anywhere.

With so many different priorities, there is inevitably a lot of "hurry up and wait," when people spend tremendous amounts of strenuous effort to get something done by a deadline only to have the organization decide to take a pause for some reason. The pause often can turn into a death for the initiative when, potentially weeks or months later, people all of a sudden think, "Whatever happened to initiative X? That was such a huge priority for so long, and now it seems to have vaporized. Weird."

A company that tries to do too much also typically commits the critical flaw of Unclear Goals, which you probably just read about in the previous chapter. Specifically, they often have a problem with layer three of that flaw: goals that aren't aligned or shared across multiple functions or regions. All the symptoms that go with that flaw can happen as well.

TREATING DOING TOO MUCH

A great example of a company that solved the issue of doing too much is Apple. No company focuses better than Apple.

According to Walter Isaacson, when Steve Jobs returned to Apple in the late 1990s, he saw that the company was working on so many projects that nothing was really getting accomplished. And nothing great was being developed.

He made everyone stop what they were doing and refocused them on creating ideas for only four quadrants of products (desktop personal, desktop commercial, mobile personal, mobile commercial). That focus is what led Apple to create the new iMac, as well as the iPod and iPhone. Steve Jobs recognized that it's best to focus on only a few of the truly best ideas (consistent with the company's strategy and purpose) and then execute them beautifully.

The Navy SEALs, who must move extremely fast in the

situations they face, have a saying: "Slow is smooth, smooth is fast." What this means is that before they execute a maneuver or an operation at full speed, they first do it very slowly and then progressively get faster until they can do it automatically at full speed.

Companies can apply this philosophy to the initiatives they choose for the year and the way in which they execute on initiatives. Once they decide the few key things they're going to focus on, they should methodically work cross-functionally to establish how they're going to go about doing them. They should think through all the areas that might be a problem and create contingency plans.

This is the slow that leads to smooth and fast. Once the plans and contingencies are developed, then they should execute the plan. But many organizations don't understand this and continually fall into the trap of trying to do everything they think is a good idea, thus moving too fast and stretching resources way too thin.

Solving this issue requires a significant mind shift for senior company leaders like you.

Take inspiration from Steve Jobs again..."People think focus means saying yes to the thing you've got to focus on. But that's not what it means at all. It means saying no to the hundred other good ideas that there are. You have to pick carefully. I'm actually as proud of the things we haven't done as the things I have done. Innovation is saying no to 1,000 things."

"Pick carefully." What does that mean? How do you do it? In my experience, it means no more than three to five initiatives per year for the company. Period.

It's going to be tempting to try and squeeze in one more. Or a few more. Or to say, "Let's expand it and do ten initiatives." But remember, doing a few things brilliantly is much better than doing many things at "good enough" just to say you've done them.

And what kind of initiatives are you looking to prioritize? Obviously, the ones that will make the biggest impact, but what does that mean? Remember that the best initiatives are the ones that genuinely "add value" for your customers.

What does it mean to "add value?" Very simply, as we saw in the blind spots chapter, it means making your customers' lives easier—however you can—by fixing what they hate and what causes them pain. That's it.

THE "VITAL FEW RETREAT"

Walter Isaacson writes that each year Steve Jobs would host a retreat for his top executives where they would decide, from all the ideas, what they were going to focus on for the year.

This is an easily replicable idea that any company can implement. I call it the "vital few retreat."

All you have to do is pick the dates and place. Then, have every leader bring their best ideas to the meeting, and have the CEO preside (along with a neutral, external facilitator). It's also good if everyone gets to vote, which helps build consensus and motivation for people to move forward.

I've facilitated this type of workshop many times before, and it's worked brilliantly. The beauty of this workshop is that if you structure it properly, in the course of a few hours, you can easily decide on the few key things you're going to focus on for the year that will truly change the game or have the most impact.

The best compliment I ever received when conducting one of these sessions was when I worked with a team to narrow down more than one hundred initiative ideas for a year to only seven. (In my opinion, seven was still too many, but it was certainly great progress.) Several people came up to me after the session to thank me.

One particular executive said, "You know…that session was really great. I loved it. I can't believe how well it worked. When I heard about the fact that we were going to have this session at our meeting, I thought, 'Oh, my God, this is going to be SO painful!' But it wasn't painful at all. In fact, it was invigorating. I can't believe you were able to help us focus so well and so fast. Thank you! Great job!"

One key to making this meeting successful is to make sure that anyone coming to the meeting with ideas has a reasonable understanding of how much value the idea will generate. That way, they can articulate and show it when there is debate. So these workshops require pre-work from the invited top leaders.

The invited top leaders should ask their teams for ideas as part of this process. In fact, the process is replicable throughout the organization and can begin from the bottom up. This is probably the most effective way to do it.

Every function or region can have a meeting like this, which then becomes the subject of the vital few retreat.

It's key during the retreat (and in all the meetings leading up to it, as well as most other meetings, really) to have people moving around, lots of flip charts, sticky notes with ideas, presenting ideas, voting on ideas, until you prioritize the vital few. Then, have the top leaders and CEO make the final decision.

And remember, no more than three to five priorities in a year!

Once the top initiatives for the year are decided in the executive meeting, then the executives can use the rest of the retreat to plan how each department will contribute to those initiatives cross-functionally and get them done, including contingency plans for what may go wrong or what obstacles may come up and how to address those things.

By doing this "vital few retreat" at the beginning of the year (or whenever the beginning of your business cycle is), you will ensure that your company has a clear focus and does not do too much by having a bunch of unnecessary siloed goals. Then, you just need to execute and stick to your guns. Resist the temptation to keep adding things or change course as the year progresses and distractions, noise, and shiny objects present themselves.

Going back to the beginning of this chapter, one way to help yourself resist the temptations is to change your own environment and situation. Start by shutting off your phone and paying complete attention during important meetings and conference calls!

KEY TAKEAWAYS FROM THIS CHAPTER

- Stop doing too many initiatives at once.

- Host a "vital few retreat" at the beginning of the year to prioritize no more than three to five initiatives.

- Focus everyone in the company on the vital few.

- Stick to your guns and don't stray from the vital few.

DYSFUNCTIONAL INFRASTRUCTURE

"It is difficult to get a man to understand something, when his salary depends on his not understanding it."

—UPTON SINCLAIR

This chapter deals with the biggest part of the environment and situation, which is the company infrastructure. Of all the critical flaws presented in this book, this one might be the keystone.

Above and beyond everything else, so many of the problems in a company truly are caused by the company's infrastructure. To fix your problems, you may need to completely redesign your organization.

TYPES OF INFRASTRUCTURE

As Thomas Gilbert's Behavioral Engineering Model

and Paul Elliott's Exemplary Performance System show, all companies have a variety of types of infrastructure, including the following:

FORMAL REPORTING STRUCTURE/ ORGANIZATIONAL CHART

This, of course, lists who reports to whom and what everyone's title is. Most organizations have a "functional" infrastructure based around the different functions of the company—for example, marketing, sales, or operations. All the people who work in each department report to their functional leader.

This type of infrastructure is common because it is easy to digest and because it is necessary on some levels. For example, junior-level staff in a marketing organization may need a functional marketing leader to help them choose better strategies and tactics based on having more marketing experience and so forth.

But often this type of functional infrastructure means that the work being done in each function is separate and siloed. No doubt you have heard someone say, "Our organization is very siloed." You may have heard it or feel that way about your company.

The problem with this type of siloed infrastructure is

that most processes in a company—especially the really important ones—involve multiple if not most functions, and without organizational structure that considers all necessary functions, there will be trouble.

COMPENSATION AND RECOGNITION

Here's where the Upton Sinclair quote is literally correct. How people are compensated is a huge determinant of what they will do and what they will not do, especially when it comes to changing their behavior. People may be fully trained on how to do something in a new and different way. They may believe that it's the right thing to do and want to do it. But if they are not paid to do it that way, they probably won't.

"Paid" could mean salary, but more than likely it means bonus. In companies that give bonuses, employees who are eligible care about things and put effort toward things that will get them their bonus. If you haven't figured out a way to incorporate the company goals (hopefully shared) or the new way of doing things into everyone's bonus or salary to compensate them for doing it, that's a problem.

Even worse, some organizations ask and expect people to do things differently even when their bonus and/or salary still depends on them doing it the old way. Then the leaders are surprised and annoyed when the change fails and people don't do it. This leads to a lot of scape-goating of people, as discussed earlier.

Think the people in your company "just don't like change?" Don't hire a whole bunch of change management experts or put people through change management training. Change their compensation structure to be based on the new way and watch the magic happen.

Aside from financial compensation, recognition is another piece that can make or break a change and is a central part of what people do or don't do. If people are not recognized (formally and informally) for doing something in a new way or achieving the new company goal(s), then they probably won't do it the way you want them to.

The inverse of this is also true. If there are no negative consequences (like disciplinary action, not getting a bonus or full salary, or getting a bad performance review) for doing things the old way, then there's no reason people really need to change, and they probably won't—especially since they already know the old way, so it's easier for them to just do that.

EXPECTATIONS AND FEEDBACK

Lots of articles and literature these days talk about the importance of companies having "performance management" or a "performance management system." This usually means having software that enables your company to have a place to put in goals and performance review information for everyone. It may do a variety of other things as well, which is fine.

But I'm not talking about that. Certainly, it's fine and generally necessary to have that. But if that's the only time people give expectations and feedback in your company, and there is no system or process for how to set expectations and give feedback on a much more regular basis, then it's not surprising that your company performance is bad.

And please note that I'm not talking about expectations and feedback related to following the company values. While it's great to have overarching shared company values (like honesty, integrity, productivity, and so on) or competencies (like results orientation, critical thinking, communication, or collaboration), those values are so broad and general that it's ridiculous to try to set expectations and give feedback to people on them.

As an example, I have a friend who worked at a company where one "competency" that people were formally evaluated on was "Living the Values." There were only two options—you either met expectations or you didn't. It was a silly checkbox that no one took seriously and actually damaged the integrity of the feedback process.

TOOLS AND RESOURCES

The final element of infrastructure to consider here is what kind of tools and resources people have to do their jobs and produce desired valuable outputs for the company. Certainly tools and resources includes technology, which is a critical flaw in itself, but I'm going to save that for later in the book. In this case, I'm talking about any other tools or resources that people have or don't have that either enable them to do things the best way or work against them doing things the best way.

Sometimes, there are tools (like Excel spreadsheets, calculators, signal readers) and resources (like job aids, operating manuals, knowledge bases) that are extremely helpful for ensuring a task is done correctly. In many cases, however, companies either have a tool or resource that isn't the best for doing the task—or they don't actually have a tool or resource for doing the task.

As with compensation and recognition, even if people are trained on how to do a task and want to do a good job, without the proper tools and resources accessible when they need them and in the way they need them, they probably won't succeed. At best, they will be okay, but not great.

Note that sometimes a resource could be something that everyone would take for granted, like a second computer monitor or an ergonomic chair. Tools and resources are highly dependent on the specific task that needs to be done.

SYMPTOMS OF A DYSFUNCTIONAL INFRASTRUCTURE

Lots of symptoms show themselves when a dysfunctional infrastructure exists in an organization. These include:

SILOED WORK AND RESULTS

Different functions tend to do their own thing and aren't aware of what other functions are doing. This can lead to mixed results in a company where one function or region does well while others do not. In the best case, there may not be too much harm.

But often it leads to a case of employees not communicating about things they need to communicate about—because everyone is just working in their silos. Employees and (perhaps worse) customers can often perceive that lack of communication as anywhere from funny and silly to downright detrimental—a case of somehow "the right hand is not talking to the left hand." This often leads to the next symptom (which is a symptom here but also was our first critical flaw): finger-pointing and politics.

FINGER-POINTING AND POLITICS

This happens, of course, when things go wrong and goals are not met—especially by cross-functional teams that aren't officially on the org chart. For example, when someone asks why a deadline was missed or why a project wasn't completed to an appropriate level of quality, people will say, "It's marketing's fault." They pin it on a certain function, especially if that function was not on the committee or was not a strong cross-functional team participant.

Another form of politics that comes from this is people who want to gain power by absorbing leadership of a different function. They see that one function needs some help or is not able to do what they need to in the way they need to. Based on that, they may intentionally make it more difficult for that function in order to "let them fail," so others will see weakness and they can come in and do a power grab.

Of course, the customers get lost in these power dynamics, which is what can be so damaging. What's more, if there is finger-pointing and politics as well, that will obviously affect employee engagement.

LACK OF EMPLOYEE ENGAGEMENT

Anytime there is an employee engagement survey done in

a company, there is always a question that asks employees how well connected they feel (and sometimes also how well connected their managers and company leadership make them feel) to the company's purpose. When there is a dysfunctional infrastructure that is siloed and not aligned, it becomes very difficult for employees to understand and feel connected to how they are really helping the company and how all the different siloes are interrelated.

I once had a colleague who worked for a company that had a very siloed infrastructure. The senior leaders knew they needed to get people in the company to work better together and be more aware of what was going on in all parts of the company. So, as often happens, they scapegoated. They decided they were going to create a training to help the situation.

They put more than a thousand people through a one-day training involving a case study that was related to a problem the company was having. Although the training was well designed and relevant to what was going on in the company, and several people said the training was interesting, it was fascinating that the majority of people who were in the training said it was a waste of time because it didn't relate to what they actually did every day. After the training, since there was no change to the siloed infrastructure, everyone went back to their silos, and nothing different happened.

DISSATISFIED CUSTOMERS

In this case, the root of the dissatisfied customer is often because of bureaucracy created by the dysfunctional infrastructure. How many times have you tried to get help from a company only to be told by the first line support that they can't really help you? They may say, "I'm sorry, but that's not my department. I need to transfer you to the XYZ department." Then what usually happens? You get transferred, and the person who picks up knows nothing about your issue (they are in a different department, of course!), so you need to repeat your entire story again.

How frustrating is that as a customer? I know you've had this happen to you. It probably happens a lot in your company, too. Again, in a case like this, the issue is not that the employee is bad and doesn't want to help—or even that the process is bad. It's that they can't beat the company's dysfunctional infrastructure.

Remember the Geary Rummler quote, "When you put good people up against a broken system, the broken system wins almost every time." Here it is in action.

In fact, have you noticed that many of the great customer service examples often involve employees who go out of their way to break company policy and infrastructure because it's the right thing to do? Isn't that crazy? The role of the company (and your role as a senior leader) should be to make it easy for service to be great. If a story like that has ever happened in your company, then you know you need to fix your dysfunctional infrastructure.

GOALS NOT BEING MET OR DEADLINES BEING MISSED

When the parts of a company's infrastructure do not function well together, it is very difficult to achieve goals and meet deadlines. Anytime your company is not achieving its goals (assuming they are not Unclear Goals), consider changing a part or parts of the company infrastructure.

INEFFECTIVE CROSS-FUNCTIONAL TEAMS

When a company org chart is not designed properly, often leaders will decide that there should be "cross-functional teams" formed from the existing parts of the organization. This is an okay idea. It's better than not doing anything.

But many times, the cross-functional teams are made up of people who also have "day jobs" in the organization that don't align with their participation on the cross-functional team. As a result of that, frequently the cross-functional team meetings aren't as productive, and employees waste a lot of time in meetings, which everyone knows is bad.

Have you ever been in (or heard about) a meeting or a

call when someone from, say, finance was supposed to be there but couldn't attend because she was "in another meeting" that she prioritized because it was part of her core function in finance? Because she was not there, you couldn't move forward with the cross-functional project. Or perhaps the team decided to make a decision without her, only to find out later that what was decided actually didn't work or caused an unanticipated problem that she would have been able to solve.

The common extension of this is that once cross-functional work is assigned, people don't complete it because it's not part of their "day job." When faced with limited time to do work, the committee members must make a critical choice. Do they do the work of their function that they officially get paid for as part of their job description and on which their performance review is based? Or, do they do the work of the committee/cross-functional team?

Of course, some people may choose to do the cross-functional work if they are very committed or if they are bonused on it. But if those things aren't there, and there is a big deadline, project, or task in their own function, that will most likely win.

And there's also the possibility that if the person tries to do everything, that will quickly lead to burnout—not to mention a whole lot of additional meetings that everyone hates.

TREATING A DYSFUNCTIONAL INFRASTRUCTURE

Remember that a company's infrastructure has four key components:

1. Formal reporting structure/organizational chart

2. Compensation/recognition

3. Expectations/feedback

4. Tools/resources

Accordingly, in order to truly cure a dysfunctional infrastructure, you need to address all four components.

FORMAL REPORTING STRUCTURE/ ORGANIZATIONAL CHART

If this flaw is deeply ingrained in your company (or if your company has a number of other flaws and symptoms that are caused by this one), then you may need to completely redesign your organization in order to cure this flaw. Please note that in this case, redesign does not mean layoffs or RIFs (Reductions In Force). The point of this redesign is not to trim the fat in the organization. It's to ensure there is official cross-functional alignment built in, so the org chart stops hindering progress.

This will allow the formalized cross-functional teams to focus on driving value for customers and innovating effectively by eliminating friction, solving customers' problems, and making their lives better. You will be happy to note that a side effect of doing this is certainly that the company is more efficient. But focusing on efficiency is not how you get there.

Cutting peoples' jobs is also not how you get there, though you will likely need to repurpose a number of people and have them do something else. That may require some additional training or support, but it will be worth it.

One of the best examples of official cross-functional structure comes from the military—specifically special operations. In the military special operations realm, every platoon has at least one person that's a specialist in each critical function (communications, navigation, medical, and so on). That way the team can function as one cohesive unit. And everyone has some knowledge of the others' functions; in case someone gets hurt or killed, this allows the team to continue.

This is a great model for the business world where most

processes involve almost all functions in an organization. Yet very few companies actually structure themselves this way.

Instead of dividing the organizational chart according to function, it's a great idea to divide it according to key business processes and involve every function that touches the process, reporting up to the process leader. For example, if "booking clients" is a key function of the business, have a dedicated senior leader of client acquisition who is responsible for the entire process including any tangential functions—everything from finding the clients and the other typical "sales" functions to the logistics associated with receiving a first payment and ensuring it's deposited properly in the bank.

On the team, make sure you have people who specialize in all steps of the process and that there is appropriate cross-training so anyone can jump in and help out if necessary. You can structure the organization this way for all key functions of the business. Again, very few companies do this, but it can really help.

COMPENSATION/RECOGNITION

Once your formal reporting structure is realigned to better serve customers and eliminate bureaucracy, the next thing you need to tackle is how people are paid and recognized. Different companies, of course, have different ways of compensating people. Here, I'm going to focus on the three core components that most companies have—salary, bonus (including any long-term incentives for those roles that have them), and merit increases for salary.

At a minimum, any bonuses should be based on achieving the newly established goals or general desired outcomes of the company. If that is not the exclusive determinant, then the overall company achieving its goals should at least play a big part in whether people get their bonus. After all, everyone is on the same team. If the company fails, then the team should fail.

Although this may seem a bit unfair, especially if there are certain people who seem to perform well, remember that the only thing that matters is whether the company achieves its goals. Giving some people a bonus (or a bigger bonus) when the company doesn't achieve its goals is just going to lead to politics and finger-pointing. In addition to a bonus, merit increases should also be tied to achieving company goals and should be an "everyone wins or no one wins" scenario.

Each person's performance evaluation, which should affect their merit increase (and hopefully bonus potential), should be tied to how well they uphold the standards and processes that contribute to the company doing well. (For a detailed description of standards and processes, see the next chapter on SOPs, which clarifies how everything should align back to compensation.)

As for salary, most of the time there is a range for each position in the company. Along the same lines as the performance evaluation and merit increase, ideally the people who produce the best results by upholding the standards and processes best should have the highest salaries.

Many companies pay people more for their experience and background. This is fine as a starting point. But at the end of the day, employee performance is not about potential or what someone brings to the table. It's about what they leave on the table—their work product. The more there is transparency around what the desired outcome is, the easier it is to pay people commensurate with the outcomes they produce.

Now, take everything I said and apply it to recognition. People (and, more importantly, teams) should be recognized, formally and informally, for achieving desired company results and properly following standards and processes. If they are not following processes, then they need to be coached or disciplined, unless they can show that their way of doing things is even better. Then that's really a cause to celebrate and then replicate that by making it the new standard for everyone to follow.

Just make sure that before you coach or discipline someone, you are crystal clear on the desired outcome they need to produce and the things they need to do to produce it.

Finally, remember that if you don't have proper SOPs and desired outcomes, you can't blame the people for performing poorly. The processes a company does are another part of its infrastructure. But since they are so detailed and critical—and a lot of companies approach them in a flawed way, we are treating them separately from the rest of the company infrastructure. As the next chapter shows, no SOPs is a critical flaw in and of itself.

EXPECTATIONS/FEEDBACK

There need to be expectations set and an infrastructure in place that everyone in the company is aware of for how to set expectations and how to give feedback, not only on peoples' performance objectives or goals but also on the specifics of the regular "day job" work they do. It's so important to set the expectation about this that I would recommend it being set by HR and (even better) you and the company executives as part of someone's immediate onboarding.

Yes, the actual feedback that each employee gets will happen within each person's job in the business function the person is a part of. But having HR and senior leaders talk about it clearly in the first days of someone's employment as a central theme of the overall company is very powerful and sets an immediate tone and expectation.

Really, you want to communicate the honest truth about why there is honest feedback, which is: you want the person to be successful in their role by producing desired outcomes for the company. Regular, precise feedback helps them do that. Of course, in order to truly be able to give appropriate feedback, you need proper SOPs.

As you may have guessed, it's not enough just to give people a performance review once or twice a year. As long as there are clear desired outcomes, proper SOPs, and a general expectation that managers and leaders should expect to give their people regular feedback, then giving the feedback is actually pretty easy and should not be controversial.

One of the best ways to build this into the culture is to have regular check-ins with each of your direct reports. Depending on the circumstances, these may be daily, weekly, every two weeks, or every month. But any less frequently than that is probably a bad idea.

Again, if the desired outcomes, standards, and procedures are clear, then the regular check-in probably doesn't need to be very long—especially for people who are performing well and producing the desired results. In that case, the check-in is probably more of a "Great job! Thank you for all you do! What else do you need from me?" type of discussion. If someone is not performing well, then the check-in is a time for them to be reminded of the SOPs and observed by the manager with the aim of diagnosing why they are not able to follow the SOP and then coaching them to get there.

Many companies have real trouble instilling this kind of process throughout the organization. The reason is that it doesn't happen at all levels. So as a senior leader, make sure you are also having regular check-ins with your direct reports—even though they are very senior people. Hold the people below you accountable for doing it with their direct reports as well, and on down the chain. Sometimes all you have to do is regularly ask your direct reports how the check-ins with their team are going. By knowing that's a regular question you always ask, they will come prepared, which means they will have done it.

TOOLS/RESOURCES

Even if you have an appropriate formal reporting structure, fully aligned compensation and recognition, and strong mechanisms for setting expectations and giving relevant, helpful feedback, you still need to make sure that people have the tools and resources they need to get the job done.

There is no one size fits all. Tools and resources are highly dependent on the specific task and desired outcome. So listen to your people. Ask them if they have everything they need or if there is something they wish they had that would help them do the job better. Better yet, as you redesign the work of the people in the company, brainstorm the tools and resources people will need to do an outstanding job.

Ideally, learn from the top performers who are already successful. Whatever tools and resources they are using, make sure everyone has them. This could be simple, obvious stuff like standing desks, extra computer monitors, or a quiet place to work (which is definitely a resource that a lot of companies are stupidly stingy with). Or it could be a specific tool that people need at some point in the process of doing the tasks to get the job done.

Make sure you consider everything.

What may seem silly or inconsequential to you may be the key to someone's success.

KEY TAKEAWAYS FROM THIS CHAPTER

- Dysfunctional infrastructure is often the deepest root cause of poor performance in your company, but few people think of it or have the courage to truly address it.

- Redesign all parts of your company infrastructure to eliminate friction and support cross-functional collaboration that improves the lives of your customers and employees.

NO SOPs

"God, I hope Suzanne doesn't leave. No one else knows how to do what she does as well as she does. If she leaves, we're screwed."

How many times have you said something like this to yourself—or heard other people in your company say it? If this rings a bell (and especially if it happens often), then you know you have a problem with standard operating procedures (SOPs) in your company.

When I say that the critical flaw is not having SOPs, this could actually be caused by one of two possibilities: either (1) there really are no defined SOPs for key functions of the business; or (2) the processes, procedures, and standards are poorly developed or documented. Either way, it's a big problem.

If a particular process is critical for business success, then it's also critical that the process be properly documented. Effective processes (and documentation) are a huge key to consistent successful performance and are essential for scalability.

If a process does not exist or is not documented, then chances are only one person or a handful of people know how to do it. If they leave, as you know, you're in trouble.

EXCUSES AND REALITY

So why don't more companies have better designed and documented processes? There are many reasons, but usually, they're just poor excuses. Here are the excuses I always hear. All of them are bad.

Excuse #1: Focusing on processes and documentation is too detail-oriented and boring.

Reality Check. Just because you don't like it doesn't mean it shouldn't be done. There are a lot of people in your company, and the success of your company depends on all of them doing things consistently and effectively.

If you personally don't like process or details, that's fine. Hire someone who does. Or, better yet, have a team of people who focus on this. Your company will be better for it.

Just don't pretend that your lack of interest means it's unimportant or unnecessary. And don't underestimate the importance of it.

Excuse #2: No one will ever use the documentation, especially if it's too detailed.

Reality Check. Yes, they will. At least, the vast majority will, and that's what matters. People want to be successful in their jobs. If your processes are well designed and documented, they will be.

I have created lots of processes and process documentation in my time—even in the face of this excuse. Every time, the people who were actually doing the work were extremely grateful and said they desperately needed what I gave them. The best analogy I can think of is that they soaked it up like sponges.

They posted the documentation in their offices and cubes, shared it with each other, called it up on their computers, and referenced it when they needed to. Their managers also used it to observe them and help them. And they were able to help each other whenever they needed it. Overall, it's always been a positive.

It is important to note that once people become competent performers at whatever process they are performing, then some of them may not need the documentation forever. But they at least will need it at the beginning. For some things (like tasks that are very complicated, have a high cost of error, and/or are not done often enough to be memorized), they will always need it—and they will actually probably always want it.

By the way, having great process documentation is an effective way to cut down on training costs, since people can just be trained to find the right process document and follow it rather than having to sit through some long, drawn-out training.

Excuse #3: We aren't really sure what the best process is or what the process should be.

Reality check. This means you might need to put some brainpower into it first. But it doesn't mean you shouldn't focus on it. In fact, you probably should focus on it right away so you can figure it out and get it documented and scaled.

A great place to start is with your star performers who are already doing a great job. If you don't have any of those for a particular role or process, then think about the outcomes you want and begin the process development and documentation with your team anyway—as shown in the Treatment section of this chapter below.

Excuse #4: Too much focus on process will cause people to be "robots" who will:

- Lose their critical thinking and problem-solving skills

- Just do what they're told to do explicitly based on some checklist

- Lose accountability for results as long as they are checking the boxes on the checklist

Reality Check. This is a gross exaggeration and unlikely to happen. Consider the opposite and realize that the cost of not having effective processes and documentation is far greater than any costs associated with having them.

If any of these "robot" conditions does happen, it's probably not because of the process or documentation. More than likely, if you have people who don't think or solve problems, who just do what they are told, and who have no accountability as long as they follow a checklist, then your company has other critical flaws that need to be dealt with. So make sure you read this entire book!

However, there is a small nugget to be aware of. If the process and documentation are not done properly, then people may feel like they are doing what they need to but still not succeeding.

I was working with a particular corporate department that had a relatively new leader named Jake. Jake had taken over the department after Sally, the previous leader, had to move on because she was no longer effective.

Sally had been a staunch checklist advocate and, when the department performed poorly, some people on the team had taken to giving the excuse that it wasn't their fault because they had followed Sally's checklists. Because of this, Jake swung the pendulum in the complete opposite direction. He eliminated all the checklists and let people do whatever they wanted.

As you can imagine, chaos ensued as there was no consistency among the team. A few people did a good job; others were terrible. Most were somewhere in the middle. It was very much a bell curve.

Customers started to complain and leave. When I approached Jake about this and suggested he needed better processes and documentation, he said, "No way. I know what happened when Sally was here. She was too process focused, and it killed everything, including everyone's morale. We are not going back to that."

After many conversations, we were able to fix the situation. I'll explain the details of how in the Treatment section later in the chapter. But the primary theme was that we made sure the process documentation had all the components it needed to have, which the previous checklists did not.

Perhaps the biggest reason why companies don't do a better job with SOPs is that they don't really know how to do a better job (or there is no person or team in the company who really specializes in this that can help them). A company may have checklists and processes, but if they don't cover the right things, then they will inevitably wind up somewhere on the continuum between mildly useless and downright harmful.

Excuse #5: Employees will lose all creativity and never innovate if they're just following the process.

Reality Check. Your employees who are doing critical processes don't want to be creative innovators—at least not right away. As a senior executive, you don't want people in your company to be creative innovators either.

What your employees really want is to be successful. You, too, just want them to be successful because that means they will produce the results you need. Having strong processes is what enables them to do that. Being creative innovators may not enable them and may actually distract them from what they need to do to be successful.

Once you have well defined and documented processes that lead to the kind of successes and outcomes you want, then you can iterate and innovate over time. Many more people will be able to contribute to the innovation, since everyone will be on the same page about the best current way to do the critical process.

As another thought on this, recognize that not having any strongly defined and documented processes, allowing employees to come up with their own (under the guise of fostering creativity and innovation), is like handing typewriters to monkeys and expecting them to write coherent sentences. A few might figure it out, but most won't.

If that doesn't convince you, then think about this...If you already have a lot of people in that role, why are they all getting different results? See what I mean?

I was working with another corporate department that was concerned about making sure they got creativity out of their team in lieu of having them follow effective processes. To do this, they had one day per month that was designated as "Genius Day."

The concept was "anyone can be a genius, so let's give everyone an opportunity to be one." On Genius Day, anyone in the department that had an idea for an innovation was able to come to the event and share their idea with everyone else in the room. If everyone liked the idea, then it would be implemented.

Now, this is a nice concept for employee morale, and it certainly made some people feel like their ideas were heard. But otherwise, it was a total disaster.

None of the key department leaders ever went to Genius Day. It was generally only the same few middle managers who were assigned to go.

The people bringing new ideas were generally the same few average-performing individuals who really only loved hearing themselves talk and getting out of doing their work for a little while, plus a few new hires who felt obligated to go and voice their opinions even though they were still really new.

None of the superstar performers ever went to Genius Day. They were all busy doing their work, which was already great—even though not everyone paid a lot of attention to them.

The real problem was that the middle managers who presided over Genius Day would take whatever ideas were presented and run with them. They would decide that whatever ideas were presented that day would work.

So every time Genius Day happened, there would be a new direction. No one could figure out where it came from. All of a sudden, there would be a strong sense of urgency to roll something out immediately—even though it had never been vetted by the department leadership.

All in the name of having everyone be heard and fostering "innovation." I can't even begin to describe the unnecessary work that was created because of this.

The biggest (and most sobering) thing to learn from Genius Day is that, unfortunately, not everyone is a genius. The majority of the ideas came from people who were known as average performers, who were suggesting that the department make their average processes the standards for everyone. Because the middle managers wanted to do their part and make everyone feel good, these unvetted, average ideas were immediately "fast-tracked" to be implemented.

Fortunately, on most occasions, they eventually petered out, but not without a lot of effort and wasted work and time.

Some ideas did get through and become "standard," which confused everyone and made them struggle—except for the star performers, who knew better and just ignored these bad ideas. (Note, though, that "standard" is a loose term here, as this department did not really have standards or processes that were enforced; everyone was always encouraged to "do their own thing.")

Because of this generally innocent, well-intentioned idea of Genius Day, this department almost succeeded at scaling average performance—not something you want to repeat and scale in your company.

Make sure that when you have a process, it's the best it can be and produces the result you need or want, even if it doesn't seem that exciting, creative, or innovative.

Excuse #6: Process documentation is too hard to update. It's another thing we have to worry about.

Reality Check. With today's technology and methods, it does not need to be difficult to update process documentation. If you assign the responsibility appropriately, it can get done easily.

Also, bear in mind that process documentation is not just something extraneous to worry about. It's really at the heart of delighting your customers and preventing costly and embarrassing errors. So give it the attention it deserves.

QUESTIONS FOR DIAGNOSIS OF NO SOPs

Not sure how to determine if lack of proper process or documentation is happening in your company? Below is a list of diagnostic questions.

If you answer yes to most or all of these, you know your company has this critical flaw. Even if you only answer yes to one or a few of these questions, you may still need to address the issue.

Before asking these questions, however, let's make sure it's not obvious by asking this one direct question: Does your company have existing SOPs that you and everyone else know about and use—for all core and supporting processes?

If it does, then look at the questions below to make sure everything about them is appropriate and that you're not just saying yes out of instinct. If it doesn't, then you obviously have this critical flaw, and you need to fix it.

You should still look at the questions below, though, to give you context. You'll probably recognize many if not all of the symptoms associated with them.

1. Are you worried that if a few key people in certain areas (or a number of different areas) leave, your company will really suffer?

2. Are you very concerned about "succession planning" and that there is not a strong bench of talent in your company? (Note that succession planning is conceptually important, and you should do it, especially at higher levels in your company. But it's often more important to have well defined and documented processes than succession planning.)

3. Does everyone in a certain role do things differently and with varying degrees of success?

4. Do most people in your company get "meets expectations" in their performance review—even if the company is not doing well and there is a sense that some people are not as good as others?

5. Do your employees complain that certain managers are very particular while others are not—and that it's unfair?

6. Do your employees complain that their performance reviews are very subjective and/or based on whether their manager "likes them or not?"

7. Are supervisors and managers struggling with having effective one-on-ones, check-ins, or performance conversations with their teams—or just not doing them?

8. Are you or are certain people/departments in your company trying new ways of doing things seemingly every day, week, or month?

9. Does it feel to you or your employees like there's always a "flavor of the month" fad you're trying to implement that's constantly changing?

10. Are you letting anyone come up with new ideas and initiatives and then rolling them out as quickly as possible without really vetting them—just to see if they stick?

11. Are your customers complaining that some people in your company are good but others are not—and then requesting to deal only with those who are good?

Again, the more yes answers you gave to the above questions, the deeper this flaw is ingrained in your company.

TREATING NO SOPs

There are three key ways to treat this flaw:

1. Focus on outcomes and sign-off tests

2. Benchmark your top performers

3. Cover all the bases

Most companies don't do any of these things. It is a game changer when they do.

And what's nice about these things is that they make everything very simple and clear. They distill a lot of information, thoughts, and feelings into their tangible essence.

In fact, when you see the finished product of your work around this—a proper SOP—you will likely say to yourself, "Wow. That seems so obvious and clear." And yet it never existed until you did it and were finally able to put into crystal clear words (for everyone to see) that which some people (but not everyone) innately understood or felt but could not really articulate.

FOCUS ON OUTCOMES AND SIGN-OFF TESTS

An outcome is a product you produce. Paul Elliott and his predecessors in the human performance technology space call this an "accomplishment." It is a noun—a person, place, or thing.

Sometimes it's easy to know what your product is. If you run a manufacturing company that produces widgets, then the outcome you're looking for (obviously) is a widget. But it has to be deeper than that.

What you have to do is incorporate an adjective, adjective

phrase, or descriptor that describes the widget in terms based on a standard that proves the outcome is correct or successful. That is the real outcome you are looking for. So in the case of a widget, your real outcome would likely be something like:

- A finished widget

- A defect-free widget

In the case of a service business, your outcome might be something like:

- Satisfied customers

- Resolved disputes

For a doctor, the desired outcome is a "cured patient" or a "healthy person."

It is okay to have a desired outcome that is financial, such as "maximum revenue," "maximum market share," "revenue greater than budget and last year," or "greater than 30 percent profit margin." But you need to remember that often those overall financial outcomes are the result of other outcomes or accomplishments unrelated to money that ultimately lead to that overall financial outcome. For example, you may achieve the outcome of "revenue greater than budget and last year" by producing "satisfied customers" and "defect-free widgets."

In some cases, you will need to further define how you judge whether the descriptor has been achieved. I call this a "sign-off test." From the examples above, the questions that lead to the answers are: how do you know when a customer is "satisfied?" How do you know when a dispute is "resolved," when a patient is "cured," or when a person is "healthy?"

Sometimes this is hard work to think about and define. But consider this: if it's hard for you to define, how do you think the people in your company know what to do? Often, they don't. And that's why performance is so variable.

Consider most job descriptions, which generally contain a lot of verbs that talk only about what an employee should do but almost never say anything about the outcome the employee should produce. There is a big difference between telling people they should "serve customers" (note the verb "serve" that only tells people what they should do) versus telling them that they are responsible for "producing satisfied customers" and then giving them the standards for how to judge whether customers are truly satisfied.

Back to our questions...there probably are some clear

ways that you can tell if the adjective phrase/sign-off test has been achieved or not. For example, customers may pass the sign-off test and be considered "satisfied" if they volunteer (without being asked) that they appreciate the provided solution—or if they give high marks on a customer satisfaction survey. Perhaps a dispute may be considered truly "resolved" if the customer smiles at the person who helped him (or her) and says something similar to "thank you for your help," or "I feel so much better," or "I really appreciate you."

So start by writing down desired outcomes and sign-off tests for all the products and services you offer. It's critical for you to do this yourself and with your team(s). But it's also important to do one other thing—especially if you are having trouble with this: benchmark your top performers.

BENCHMARK YOUR TOP PERFORMERS

This is the "secret sauce" to how your company can succeed. Paul Elliott is the pioneer of it in his book, *Exemplary Performance*.

After reading Paul's book and consulting with him over the years, and through my own work related to this, I've learned that there really is a secret sauce inside your top performers. By using a structured process that is relatively easy to execute, you can "bottle it" and replicate it throughout your company. Here's how the process works:

1. **Figure out what the desired outcomes are for your entire company.** Use your skills from above to create the desired outcomes that include the sign-off tests. Then, do the same for each process that your company does.

    Note that you should do this for the *processes* your company does (like serving customers, acquiring customers, or collecting payment from customers), *not the functions* your company has (like marketing, sales, or finance). Remember that the overall desired outcomes for your company are composed of many other desired outcomes at lower levels.

2. **Figure out the roles that contribute most to your company's desired outcomes.** Often these are "individual contributors" (people who are just directly doing a particular role that is closely tied to the desired outcome). But they could be managers. Ultimately, you will want to benchmark top performers from any roles that contribute in a significant way to your company's desired outcomes.

3. **Figure out who the top performers are in those**

roles. They are the ones who consistently produce excellent results based on the desired outcome—above and beyond everyone else—consistently over time. If you don't know who these people are, then look at the data and find out.

After you do that, you can validate with the department leader or the direct manager or someone else who is very aware (like a corporate support leader) just to be sure. But it's always a good idea to start with data if you have it because that keeps things objective and outcome-based, which is critical.

If you don't have clear data on this, then you should start there and begin to collect it to find out who your top performers really are.

4. **Formally observe and/or interview the top performers.** There's a lot that goes into this process, so I'd recommend reading *Exemplary Performance* for the details, or hiring a consultant or team that specializes in this.

The key ingredient to the secret sauce is the mental models inside the heads of your top performers. Elliott refers to this as "covert behavior." It's essentially the way in which your top performers make decisions, which is "covert" because you can't observe how someone makes a decision just by physically looking at the person.

Note that it is generally enough just to benchmark the top performers because you know no one else is achieving those results. But if you are particularly analytical and want to prove the difference between the top performers and everyone else, you can also observe or interview some average performers as a "control" group. Doing this will definitely enable you to see the difference clearly. I've done it several times myself, and it's always fascinating to watch the bell curve of individual performance unfold before my eyes. If you're in a hurry, though, it's not necessary.

5. **Create a Profile of Exemplary Performance (PEP) or Role Excellence Profile (REP) based on the observations of the top performers.** As Paul Elliott says, a PEP or REP frames the key outcomes that the top performers produce and the tasks they do to accomplish the outcomes, which are the subjects for the SOP documentation.

6. **Create the SOP documentation.** Make sure you cover all the bases, as described in the section below.

7. **Implement the new SOPs.** Obviously, there are a lot of steps involved (probably a whole other book), so we

won't go into too much detail here. But consider the section later in this chapter called "Other applications for SOPs" as one part of implementation. Also, recognize that successful implementation of new, proper SOPs is largely dependent on curing the other critical flaws in the company, which are discussed in this book. Remember, everything is connected.

COVER ALL THE BASES

Cover all the bases means to make sure you include all key details in your SOPs. If you don't, then they won't be as useful, and that will be another problem you will need to deal with.

One of the biggest mistakes companies make with their documentation is that they list only what people need to do but not how they need to do it and how to know when it's done. That was what made Sally's checklists (from a previous story) so ineffective. As an example, if your process document looks like the following, then you are missing key details, and that's bad.

ERROR-FIXING PROCESS

Step 1. Read the error report.

Step 2. Fix errors.

Step 3. Communicate that errors have been fixed.

Looking at this example, it's pretty clear there's a lot missing, but here are some specific questions that go unaddressed:

- Where can I access the error report?

- How often do I need to read it?

- How long should it take me?

- What exactly am I looking for on the error report?

- What steps do I need to take to fix the errors?

- Are there any issues on the report or in the error-fixing process that might cause the errors to be unfixable?

- What type of communication do I need to send?

- What needs to be in the communication?

- What should not be in the communication?

- And on and on...

Even though it may be obvious here, you would be surprised how many SOPs look just like this. If you look at your company's SOPs, how many of them are too general and only cover the *what* but not the *how* or the *how to know*? While the above could certainly be fine as a quick job aid or reminder card, the actual SOP needs much more.

Proper SOP documentation has eight primary components:

1. **A specific desired outcome**. Described above.

2. **Sign-off test**. Described above.

3. **Tasks**. These are the things people need to do to achieve the desired outcome that passes the sign-off test.

4. **Triggers**. These indicate when someone should start doing each task and how often they should do it. For example, a trigger could be "every day as soon as you sit down at your desk" or "once a week, immediately after the XYZ report is produced."

5. **Duration**. This tells people how long each task should take—for example, fifteen minutes or one hour. The duration could be a range of time if that's acceptable, such as twenty to thirty minutes.

The main key here is that duration serves as a controlling factor that prevents people from either not doing enough or doing too much. And it helps managers diagnose why someone is not producing the specific desired outcome that passes the sign-off test.

As an example, if the duration of a particular task should take twenty to thirty minutes, then you know people are probably not putting in enough effort if their outcome is flawed after only fifteen minutes. Likewise, if they are taking forty-five minutes, they may be focusing on details that don't matter and actually harm the final product.

6. **Key stakeholders.** This is a list of people the worker should interact with when doing the SOP, including what type of interaction and why it's important or necessary.

7. **Decision-making flow.** This is the heart of the SOP. It's the "covert" behavior or mental model that shows people exactly what decisions they need to make and how to make them.

Very often an actual decision tree diagram is helpful in this phase. (See below for a good example.)

DECISION TREE EXAMPLE
BANK ACCOUNT MATCHING

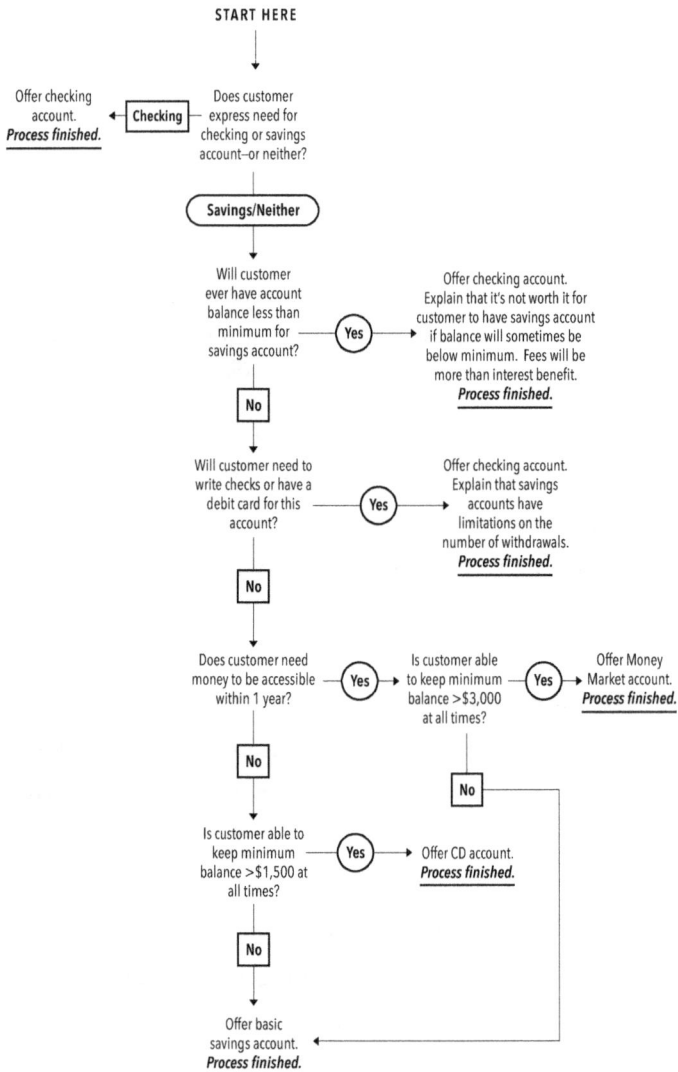

START HERE

Offer checking account.
Process finished.

┤ **Checking** ├

Does customer express need for checking or savings account–or neither?

(**Savings/Neither**)

Will customer ever have account balance less than minimum for savings account?
— (**Yes**) →
Offer checking account. Explain that it's not worth it for customer to have savings account if balance will sometimes be below minimum. Fees will be more than interest benefit.
Process finished.

[**No**]

Will customer need to write checks or have a debit card for this account?
— (**Yes**) →
Offer checking account. Explain that savings accounts have limitations on the number of withdrawals.
Process finished.

[**No**]

Does customer need money to be accessible within 1 year?
— (**Yes**) →
Is customer able to keep minimum balance >$3,000 at all times?
— (**Yes**) →
Offer Money Market account.
Process finished.

[**No**]

[**No**]

Is customer able to keep minimum balance >$1,500 at all times?
— (**Yes**) →
Offer CD account.
Process finished.

[**No**]

Offer basic savings account.
Process finished.

With a good decision-making flow, people will easily know when they are doing something right or wrong. And they will be able to work through obstacles that they encounter, thus making it seem like they have great critical thinking skills.

In fact, by following these types of decision flows, you will actually build their critical thinking skills because they will see a great model for how to think critically and make decisions. Even better, that model is automatically relevant to exactly what they are doing. And because of it, you no longer need to worry about having to send them to some generic skill-building training that offers no guarantee they will connect the dots and apply what they've generally learned to what you literally want them to do.

See what I did here? I just saved you potentially thousands of dollars in unnecessary training costs.

8. **Potential derailers, consequences, and solutions.** Every process has a variety of things that could cause it to fail. Being transparent and clear in the SOP itself about those things and the consequences they cause will help people become aware of them, spot them more quickly, and naturally work to prevent them.

By coupling the derailers and their consequences with

their potential solution(s), you will make it that much easier for people to handle problems themselves and avoid costly errors, without having to involve their managers or someone else that's higher-level. (Unless, of course, involving their manager is part of the proper solution to the derailer. In that case, it's fine.)

OTHER APPLICATIONS FOR SOPs

Once you have proper SOPs, the great news is that they are useful for a variety of things besides just being process documents that people use to do a task or process effectively.

As we already saw, they are perfect for job descriptions, which is a great place to start since that's one of the first things people see related to a particular job. I have completely redone many job descriptions very effectively and efficiently by literally cutting and pasting desired outcomes, sign-off tests, and tasks from the SOP into the job description.

Not only is this effective and efficient, but it also ensures alignment and consistency of language between your SOPs and the job description—a revolutionary concept that no one seems to think of but is really helpful for everyone (employees, managers, leaders, recruiters, and HR people) and easy to do.

Some other things that proper SOPs can be used for:

- Hiring guides and interview questions (especially case studies or behavior-based interview questions) that can be given to and used by HR or talent acquisition/recruiting.

- Training materials (classroom, online, blended) or scenarios.

- Job aids or other performance support tools.

- Coaching guides for managers to ensure that their employees are following processes effectively.

- Performance evaluation forms for documenting whether an employee's performance is up to standard or needs improvement. This really helps eliminate the perception of subjectivity in performance reviews that everyone hates and thinks is unfair. These updated forms can then be tied back to the employee compensation structure.

Again, the key here is that the SOP is the foundation that creates the common language that can be repurposed throughout the company related to the process or topic. This then creates natural alignment and shared understanding of what needs to be done and produced.

KEY TAKEAWAYS FROM THIS CHAPTER

- Stop making excuses for not being process-focused.

- Take the time to create optimal processes and document them properly.

- Repurpose your process documentation throughout your company to ensure common language, alignment, consistency, and scalability.

FIXING THE UNFIXABLE

Does your company have "nasty lists?"

I mean lists that everyone knows they don't want to be on, or they will get in trouble. Ones where the managers tell their employees, "Make sure we don't get on this list."

It could be the nasty list of people who haven't completed compliance training or the nasty list of departments that had lower same-store sales than last year. It could be the nasty list of business units that violated some company policy or went over their cost budget for the month.

I've worked with many companies that had a variety of nasty lists, underperformers, or underperforming entities. Get on a nasty list—especially more than once—and the "cavalry" would show up to do a "deep dive" to turn performance around. But often the cavalry was a group of people to whom the real workers and managers only gave lip service and then ignored, knowing that the cavalry was soon going to move on to something else.

I've seen many instances where the reason people or departments get on the nasty list is truly out of their control. For example, a hotel that is under renovation will not be able to generate as much revenue or market share as when it's not under renovation. And yet there are often meetings upon meetings and examination upon examination for those hotels—even though the cavalry's time would be better spent almost anywhere else.

Fixing the unfixable is the flaw that happens when companies devote significant resources to investigating every possible reason why some entity or person may be grossly underperforming.

It is naturally tempting whenever overall performance is down to try to figure out where exactly performance is down—which business units, cost centers, departments, regions, divisions, or people. A lot of times leaders do this so they can scapegoat and explain away poor performance by saying, "Well, even though the overall results were bad, we've isolated it to departments X and Y. If you take out the results of departments X and Y, we actually did well."

This, of course, is often just a bad excuse, though sometimes it works, because it triggers the follow-up question, "What happened to departments X and Y?" That leads to an explanation of some sort. And then, before you know it, everyone is talking about what we can do to fix departments X and Y.

But they're missing a key point. If only a few people, departments, units, or regions are underperforming, that's probably not what's driving the whole company's poor performance. Plus, there may be a clearly known reason for that underperformance (like a broken machine or hotel renovation), which can be easily explained and then deprioritized because it is not a major process, strategy, or execution issue.

One other problem with focusing only on nasty lists is what I call people being successful in spite of themselves. Especially if a company has lots of nasty lists, the thinking is that as long as you're not on a nasty list, you're performing well. But generally that's not the whole picture.

Sometimes you can be successful or stay off the nasty list even if you're not doing the right things. What gets missed here by organizations is the value that could be added by examining exactly what the people or business units/entities are doing that are not bad enough to be on the nasty list but are not excellent either. (The great middle of the bell curve.)

Research shows that significantly greater value is generated from paying attention to the high performers and replicating their performance throughout the organization than by focusing heavily on underperformers. If you really want to turn around your company's performance, stop focusing on trying to explain and fix the worst performers and instead engineer the performance curve to be what I call "right and tight."

SYMPTOMS OF FIXING THE UNFIXABLE

There are two major symptoms of fixing the unfixable: wasted time that has no real ROI and the unnecessary hard costs associated with that.

WASTED TIME

When thinking about wasted time with no ROI, here are some key questions to help you understand:

- Over the past month or year, how much time have you spent trying to fix underperformers (whether they're people or business units) to no avail?

- Over the past month or year, how many activities have you and your teams done with or for underperformers that don't change performance?

- How often do you and your team feel like you're "pissing in the wind" with underperformance?

These are true time costs that no one really thinks about, especially if you're caught up in this flaw, because you and your authority stakeholders decided you should focus on this. Cut your losses already. It's time to move on.

HARD COSTS

Now to the hard costs. If you haven't been convinced to abandon fixing the unfixable based on wasted time, maybe this will convince you. Think about the hard costs associated with having people focus so much on underperformance that can't really be prevented.

Salary costs are a big one. Below are some questions to get you started.

Salary Cost Questions

- How many meetings or calls go into managing underperformance?

- How many people are in each call/meeting?

- What level of people are involved?

- How long are the calls/meetings?

- Is there a lot of email traffic that happens as a result of this work? How long does it take a person to draft and send an email, and how long does it take a person to read each email?

- How long does it take (and how many people at each level) to create a plan to improve the significant underperformers? If there are a lot of middle and upper-middle managers involved, that really adds to the cost.

Besides salary, there are other hard costs as well.

Other Hard Cost Questions
- Is money spent on calls/meetings in addition to the associated salary cost? For example, what are the phone costs for the calls?

- Are there travel and entertainment (T&E) costs for meetings if people are flying in to discuss?

- Are there audio/visual costs for the in-person meetings?

- Are there marketing, sales, or advertising dollars

spent to try to fix these underperformers? For example, do you or your team sometimes decide to do some extra marketing to bring in extra revenue and try to offset the losses?

Hard Cost Example

In order to get a true feel for how much these hard costs add up, here's an example that's common in companies I've worked with.

Let's say there is a monthly conference call that requires ten middle managers to report to two senior leaders on the previous month's underperformers. That conference call lasts for two hours. In anticipation of the call, each middle manager must do two hours of research and strategizing to determine the cause of underperformance and come up with ideas to improve.

Then, there will be a one-day in-person meeting each quarter where two senior leaders, along with two middle managers, will fly to a destination to do a "deep dive" into the five worst performers, along with one senior leader from each of the worst performers (nine people total).

Some key statistics for this accounting:

- Average middle manager salary: $85,000 or $40.86

per hour (assuming 40 hours per week and 52 weeks per year)

- Average senior leader salary: $150,000 or $72.11 per hour

- Phone call cost: $0.05 per minute

- Flight cost per person: $500

- Hotel and transportation per night per person: $150

- Meals per day per person: $50

First, let's look at the costs associated with one conference call alone.

- One middle manager x 4 hours x $40.86 per hour = $163.44.

- Ten middle managers overall = $163.44 x 10 = $1,634.40.

- Two senior leaders = 2 hours x $72.11 per hour x 2 leaders = $288.44.

- Phone call cost = $0.05 per minute x 120 minutes (2 hours) x 12 people = $72.

- $1,634.40 + $288.44 + $72 = $1,994.84. That's almost $2,000 in costs for one two-hour call with twelve people.

Now multiply everything by 11 (since there's one every month, minus one month that may be skipped for holidays or something else). Total cost for these calls: $21,943!

More than likely, you wouldn't approve a $22,000 project without an ROI. So maybe it's time to do one on these conference calls.

Let's continue the example and add the meetings...

- Flights for 9 people: $4,500.

- Hotel and transportation for 1 night for 9 people: $1,350.

- Meals for 1 day for 9 people: $450.

- Senior leader time out of office from travel and meetings: 8 hours x 7 leaders x $72.11 per hour: $4,038.16.

- Middle manager time out of office from travel and meetings: 8 hours x 2 managers x 40.86 per hour: $653.76.

- Total cost for one meeting (including travel expenses and salary time out of office): $10,991.92.

- Total cost for 4 meetings: $43,967.78.

Based on the above examples, between conference calls and meetings alone, this is costing the company upwards of $65,000 per year. And we haven't even included other hard costs (like extra marketing, salary cost, and so on) associated with what comes out of this process. Not to mention the emotional and mental costs from people who have to spend time doing things that we all now know are not making a true impact.

So stop trying to squeeze pennies out of a rock, and let's look at what you really should be doing.

TREATING FIXING THE UNFIXABLE—"RIGHT AND TIGHT"

To fix poor performance in your company, you need to engineer the performance curve to be "right and tight."

What do I mean by "right and tight?" Two things. First, I mean that the average performers perform better than they ever have—closer to the top performers. I call this "right" because the top performers are always on the right side of the bell curve. Second, I mean that the bell curve of performance has a lot less variability. I call this "tight" because the middle of the bell is narrower than in a normal bell curve.

The incremental value from achieving a right and tight performance curve is huge. We'll look at a financial example in a moment. But for now, just think about it.

You probably have very few superstars. On the flip side, you probably also have very few truly terrible underperformers. The vast majority of people in your organization are typically somewhere in the middle. They're average.

But your company's performance can't be great if you just have a bunch of average performers. (Side note: notice I said average performers, not average people. Remember, people aren't usually the problem even if it really seems like they are).

If people were product lines, and you had three different product lines—one that sold a million units a year, one that sold 100,000 units a year, and one that sold 5,000 units a year, you wouldn't spend a lot of time and money trying to get the 5,000 unit product line to sell a million. So don't do that with your people either.

What should you do with the underperformers, you ask? Strange and hard as this may seem, you should ignore them for now. Don't worry. We'll come back to them shortly. But not until after all your flaws are cured. Because honestly right now you're just the pot calling the kettle black.

RIGHT AND TIGHT—SHOW ME THE MONEY

Let's look at the financial benefits of engineering the performance curve to be right and tight.

Think about your sales or business development team. Let's say you have sixty people on the team. Five are top performers; five are terrible, and fifty are somewhere in the middle (even if the curve is wide and middle covers a lot of ground).

Let's say the top five performers bring in an average of $400,000 each in revenue per year. The five terrible performers bring in an average of $20,000 each in revenue per year. The middle fifty bring in an average of $175,000 each in revenue per year.

Imagine if, by following the processes of the top performers, the middle fifty brought in just 20 percent more than their average (20 percent closer to what a top performer would bring in). In this case, 20 percent of $175,000 is an extra $35,000. Fifty middle performers bringing in an extra $35,000 each on an annual basis represents an incremental annual revenue of $1,750,000.

This is a huge number that could be gained for a very low cost associated with benchmarking the top performers. Why would you not do this?

Now back to the underperformers. Here's the secret: by focusing on the top and middle, you will easily be able to see why the true underperformers are underperforming.

As long as you include them on re-training and re-setting of expectations; as long as you hold them accountable for using the same tools and processes as the top performers; and so forth, it's quite likely that the underperformers may actually turn themselves around with little or no extra effort on your part. Because you will have given them the proper environment and situation to do so.

If not, or if they are underperforming because of a bad attitude even after all your company flaws have been cured, then you can and should get rid of them. But make sure you do it humanely and with dignity and support. They are probably not bad people, bad workers, dumb, or totally useless. They are just not the right fit or in the right situation at this time. So when you get rid of them, do them a favor and give them outplacement assistance to help them find their next move.

Remember Jake? The leader who didn't really want SOPs even though his department was performing poorly and needed them? After we benchmarked his top performers and proved the difference between his top performers and everyone else (after all, Jake needed proof before he was willing to truly embrace the concept and move forward), we were able to completely redesign the way his team approached their work. And there was huge progress.

Over time, his team started becoming stronger trusted advisors to their clients (which they had never really been before). The reputation of his department improved to the point where more prospective clients approached him. Because of this, his department was able to make its very aggressive growth goals, which he had previously been very scared about and was almost certain he was going to miss.

I won't pretend everything was perfect with Jake's department after this work, but the progress was undeniable. And we spent literally zero time or money trying to fix the few people who were the true worst of the underperformers.

KEY TAKEAWAYS FROM THIS CHAPTER

- Stop focusing too much on underperformance even though it is tempting to do so.

- Engineer the performance curve to be "right and tight."

LEGACY TECHNOLOGY

When I was in college, I took a class on new communication technology. This was many years ago when the internet, mobile phones, and even email were still relatively new. I remember the professor asking us a question that led to one of the most brilliant things I'd ever heard.

At the time, more people in Africa had mobile phones than people in the United States. This was amazing given that people in the US generally had a lot more disposable income than people in Africa. He asked us why we thought this situation was true. What was it that caused this situation?

A number of people tried to look smart and gave answers, but none of us got it.

"The biggest obstacle to new technology," he said at last, "is old technology." This was a revelation.

In Africa, there was no "landline" telephone infrastructure like there was in the US—nor massive companies built around it. So the African nations were among the first to rapidly adopt mobile phones, thereby leapfrogging millions of people in much more developed areas of the world. Fascinating.

Even though the world has changed tremendously since then, I've found that the concept my professor revealed that day is still true—and probably always will be. It is a big reason why many companies suffer from the flaw of legacy technology.

Legacy technology that is not replaced is holding you back much more than think. You need to bite the bullet and replace it with something that really works.

WHY DO YOU HOLD ON TO LEGACY TECHNOLOGY SO LONG?

Even though the reason above is part of the picture of why people hold on to legacy technology, there are a lot of other reasons why companies hesitate to replace their technology. Because these reasons are so ingrained in most companies—and are probably well ingrained in your mind as well—it's worth exploring them in detail.

The reason companies never prioritize replacing their

technology boils down to the fact that senior executives like you think doing so is SHIT-E. By SHIT-E, I mean: Scary, Hideous, Involved, Time-Consuming, and Erratic.

- **Scary.** This is one of the first things that comes to mind, especially if the legacy technology is a significant part of your company's infrastructure. Replacing it could interrupt the business in a big way if you're not careful. And it costs a lot of money, so if it doesn't really solve your problems, then it's a huge mistake or failure that will be very difficult to fix. That's scary.

- **Hideous.** Hideous means ugly. It's certainly possible that the process of replacing your old technology will be ugly. But in this case, I'd say hideous is really more like "unsexy."

It is definitely unsexy to replace old technology—particularly because it may prevent you from focusing on something sexier in the short term. If you replace your technology, you probably won't have budget this year (or even maybe next year) to do a whole lot else.

I vividly recall listening to one senior executive in a company I worked with explain why he was not planning to replace the company's legacy technology. He was asked the question point-blank by one daring employee at a town hall meeting.

"We have so many problems with the old system we use every day. It's so slow, and it doesn't do what we need at all," the employee said. "Are there any plans to replace it any time soon?"

The senior executive then immediately responded, without missing a beat and with great empathy. I'm sure he'd prepared for this question or, more likely, he'd heard it before (probably many times).

"Thank you for asking that question. I know it's hard to use that system and that the system is very old. But here's the thing. A new system will cost about $20 million. When I think about spending that kind of money, it becomes a choice between do I spend $20 million to buy a new system, or do I spend $20 million to launch a new product? I have to tell you that, when faced with that choice, I'm going with the new product every time."

While this was a great response in the moment from an intelligent, empathetic, experienced senior executive, it ignored the key issue that was increasingly pervasive in the company. Even though the hypothetical new product would be sexier and could generate immediate revenue, replacing the broken system is like replacing the plumbing in your building or your house. It's definitely not sexy. But you know you need to do it.

Make the hard choice and put off getting those beautiful new hardwood floors you want (but don't need) until later, after the plumbing is fixed.

If you don't replace the plumbing, you know deep down what's going to happen. At some point, the plumbing is going to fail. When that happens, there's going to be shit everywhere.

The above-mentioned executive's mentality is tied to another of the critical flaws, coming up in the next chapter: Chasing Shiny Objects. In this case, the shiny object is short-term results.

This executive knew he needed to prioritize getting as much revenue in the short term over fixing one of the company's major long-term weaknesses. The problem, of course, is that no one was paying attention to the true costs of the workaround solutions or any of the other costs and missed opportunities that were caused by the legacy technology.

· **Involved.** By this I mean complicated. When you replace legacy technology, there's a lot to think about. You need to make sure that all old functionality is accounted for or improved upon. After all, you don't want to implement something new that winds up being worse than what you had.

Then there are all the nuances of every aspect of the business that the legacy technology touches. Many times even IT departments don't know all the ramifications of what may happen when a part of the technology is changed. It can be like pulling an innocent-looking thread on a sweater only to have that sweater come completely unraveled because that thread was connected to much more than you thought.

- **Time-consuming.** This is not a surprise, and it is definitely real. Replacing legacy technology is never going to happen overnight, and it may wind up taking much longer than you originally hoped and planned for.

- **Erratic.** In this context, erratic means uncertain. It's confusing and hard to know what you should replace your legacy technology with and how to go about doing it.

Moreover, if you do replace it, there's no guarantee that the new technology will be better. It will definitely have its own set of challenges for you to deal with. Also, whatever the new technology is, you know that it's not going to last forever.

SHIFT YOUR PERSPECTIVE ON LEGACY TECHNOLOGY

There are a lot of legitimate reasons to stick with your legacy technology and, certainly, a lot of legitimate reasons why you don't want to replace it. But have you really thought about how much time and money is being spent working around your old technology?

Think of all the meetings, conference calls, pre-meeting work, post-meeting work, emails and phone calls to different departments or the IT department that owns the technology product.

Think of the bad solutions that come out of these meetings and initiatives. How much harder are they than they could be? How much time and money would be saved if your technology worked the way your company needed it to, without the friction? How much more revenue could you make based on what you currently can't do because of your legacy technology?

A great example of this occurred at the company from the previous story—the one with the empathetic senior executive. The company wanted to create a new process for a certain market segment of people to be able to book their product more effectively. They knew that if they could create this new process, this very profitable market segment of people would be happy and would generate potentially millions of dollars of incremental revenue and profit on an annual basis. But the IT infrastructure in the company was old and very well ingrained, since the company had been around for years.

With the new process, the business leaders wanted to be able to automatically flex the prices of the product each day and automatically allocate a certain amount of inventory for purchase by this market segment, based on forecasted demand. Conceptually, this is not a difficult problem and should be easy to develop and deploy given modern standards of IT infrastructure and software development.

But the existing reservations/distribution software was unable to handle that many dynamic pricing and inventory changes without potentially crashing the entire customer ordering process for all customers (not just this one market segment). The leadership team and a large cross-functional project team had to come up with a workaround.

The workaround, while eventually functional, took a huge amount of time to conceptualize and develop (about a year, in total). It consumed significant resources, including both money for development and also time from more than forty people, all of whom were well paid professionals, middle to senior-level managers, and executive leaders.

Then, when the workaround was launched, more than 2,000 people had to be trained for an hour on it because the way it functioned was so complicated and confusing. In fact, when I first heard about how the workaround would function, I laughed out loud—for a long time. It was as if a group of people had gotten together and said, "How could we make this process as confusing and hard as possible—and make sure that absolutely no one understands how it works?"

The workaround process was so convoluted that all I could do was laugh. Not only was the process extremely hard to understand and learn; but those 2000+ people then needed to spend an average of fifteen minutes per week to ensure the inventory and pricing were managed effectively. So it also gave them all yet another task. As if they needed that.

All told, including time and development costs, the company easily spent upwards of $1.1 million to develop the process and train the 2000+ staff to manage it, although no one ever really accounted for it. The workaround ensured that approximately $780,000 per year in time/salary cost would be spent managing the process moving forward.

If the IT infrastructure had been dynamic enough to allow the implementation of the original concept solution, the initial development costs probably would have been less than $100,000—and there would have been no need for 2000+ people to manage the process on an ongoing basis.

This example is just one of many similar "workaround" projects that were necessary at this company because the IT infrastructure was lacking. But no one ever really paid attention because leadership had long since given up on attempting to replace the old technology. In reality, by undertaking two or three similar projects per year, which was the norm, the company would wind up spending about $20 million in workarounds over three or four years anyway, which would easily have bought them new, better technology.

LEGACY TECHNOLOGY SYMPTOMS

This story illustrates many of the key symptoms that indicate your legacy technology should be replaced now, including:

- Lots of complaints (from employees and/or customers) about how slow or bad your systems and software are.

- Sub-optimal, extremely complex, bureaucratic, costly solutions to IT, software, process, or service problems that are conceptually easy to solve.

- Having to focus on IT projects that don't seem to really drive the company forward but are "necessary" to keep up.

Pseudo-Programmers

One other symptom of legacy technology is maintaining a team of "pseudo-programmers." In my experience, most companies fail to appropriately account for the value of quick, effective software development by an in-house team that understands your business. The concern is that keeping a potentially large team of software developers on staff is expensive and potentially unnecessary, especially given the prevalence of SaaS (Software as a Service) vendors in the world today.

While this may be the case in some (likely smaller) companies that can easily rely on off-the-shelf software that's effective for their business purpose, most companies are large enough and their business complex enough that off-the-shelf software is not adequate and will need to be customized in some way. This is especially true if the company has other pieces of existing software that need to be integrated in some form.

Here's where we land on this final symptom. Most companies that have complex software systems, businesses, and integrations inevitably wind up having some type of internal team that does pseudo-programming, which is one or two steps below actual software coding. They do their pseudo-programming in applications like Tableau, Microsoft Excel, Microsoft Access, or even SQL, where they create tools and reports that integrate outputs or information from different software applications. They do this type of pseudo-programming work so people in the company can get something that's actually useful and actionable from all the nonintegrated data they have that doesn't naturally flow together.

These pseudo-programming teams (which are often called business analysis teams or business intelligence teams or some such name) typically exist only because the software applications don't properly talk to each other. And, ultimately and most importantly, because the software doesn't truly meet the business's needs.

Since it's "too hard" to develop software in a way that truly meets changing business needs, the company winds up establishing a team whose responsibility it is to develop clunky, low-tech workarounds. But this is very inefficient and typically very frustrating for the business team that's trying to compete better, especially with a competitor that is nimbler in the software development area—or even with a large company that has technology as a core competency.

Let's not forget that the team of pseudo-programmers

costs a lot of money to keep and is part of the FTE count, so this symptom is particularly costly, too.

TREATING LEGACY TECHNOLOGY

The key to overcoming this flaw is really just to bite the proverbial bullet and make the decision to replace the old technology with something new and scalable. In order to make this happen, you will need a solid business case that shows it's necessary and has a positive ROI. When building this case, make sure to account for all the "workaround" projects that happen in any given year at the company, which will help show the true ROI of replacing your legacy technology. Account for these elements:

· Time spent for each person on the planning and implementation teams.

· Actual software development costs and/or hardware costs.

· Training and communications for the workarounds.

· Costs (both time and money) associated with any ongoing new processes that will have to be implemented and managed as a result of the workarounds.

Also account for how much faster existing processes

could move if the IT infrastructure were replaced. And how much faster new products or services could get to market if the IT infrastructure were not an issue. These things can benefit both your revenues and your costs, depending on what you're doing.

MORE PROGRAMMERS

While you're at it, make a strategic investment in technology for your company by hiring more programmers/developers/coders who develop actual software applications, rather than just visualizations or analysis. Although it may not always seem like it, I consider these people to be like Special Operations warriors. They have the potential to be a "force multiplier" on your "battlefield" if they can quickly develop effective, integrated software solutions that enable you to get new products or services to market faster—or to more efficiently or effectively iterate your existing processes without getting mired in costly, frustrating, suboptimal workarounds.

An in-house software team may not enable your company to completely eliminate vendors, but it likely means that there will be much less reliance on them and more effective and efficient changes in software to meet changing business needs.

If you're concerned that there won't be anything for the

programmers to do after they replace or fix your legacy technology, don't be. That will never happen. If you're worried that you may go crazy and hire too many of them, thus making your FTE count look bloated or reaching a point of diminishing returns, forget that. You're looking at it wrong.

I've literally never heard anyone in any company say that there is nothing else they need from the software development team. In fact, in every company I've ever worked with, it's the opposite. The chief complaint is always, "I wish we had more developers/programmers so we could get more stuff developed faster. It's so frustrating that we can't get things developed as fast as we need them. If we only had better technology, we could do so much more!"

FINAL THOUGHTS

Remember that even though it will likely be expensive and difficult to replace your legacy technology, eventually there will be a payback. It will probably come sooner than you expect, since there won't be so many workarounds and all the baggage that comes with them (unless, of course, you have other critical flaws that remain unaddressed).

By replacing your legacy technology and investing strategically in a skilled team of software developers, you can finally get the technology solutions you need to ease your customers' pain, make their lives better, and leapfrog your competition.

Now that I'm more experienced, I can clearly say that my old college professor, smart as he is, was wrong. The biggest obstacle to new technology actually is not old technology. It's people. People who are hesitant to change and are afraid of or unwilling to make the leap to something better because they are worried about or don't want to deal with the journey.

The good news is you no longer have to be one of those people. You have the ability to make the change in your company. And by making the change, even though it is risky and could fail, you likely will make a huge impact—not only on your company's bottom line but also on the lives of many of your stakeholders and their families.

With any luck, you might even create a legacy of a different kind for yourself and your company—a legacy as an innovative disruptor that changed the world.

KEY TAKEAWAYS FROM THIS CHAPTER

- Replacing legacy technology is SHIT-E. There's a risk it will fail. But you should do it.

- Hire more programmers/developers/coders. The faster they move, the faster you move.

- Replacing legacy technology is an opportunity to become a disruptor, leapfrog your competitors, thrill your customers, and potentially change the world.

CHASING SHINY OBJECTS

The phrase "chasing shiny objects" means going after whatever is the hot new thing. As a critical company flaw, it means reacting to "noise" instead of playing your game. And "noise" takes two primary forms:

- Being overly concerned with short-term quarterly results

- Reacting to the competition

In personal life, one of the worst things people can do is deal only with what comes at them rather than deciding for themselves what is important. Imagine if you spent all day only answering incoming emails without working on your goals. You would be very busy. But you would not be productive, and you would very likely not accomplish your goals.

Even starting the day by answering emails is discouraged

by many productivity experts because it puts your mind in reactive mode right away and makes you less likely to get the things done that are very important but are not coming at you. If you start your day by checking your email, you are much more likely to get sucked into the vortex that everyone knows email is.

Chasing Shiny Objects at the strategic or operational level is the corporate equivalent of spending a large portion of your day answering emails without working on your goals. Although there are a lot of shiny objects and noisy forces that may seem important and necessary to chase, they really aren't. They are just distractions.

To cure your company of this flaw, maintain clear focus on making customers' lives better and ignore these shiny objects, tempting as they may be. Just as you can take control of your email to ensure you have time to work on things that are important (e.g., by shutting off the pop-up notifications and checking email at specific times in the day), there are many things you can do to ensure you maintain control of your company and prevent shiny objects from derailing it.

BEING OVERLY CONCERNED WITH SHORT-TERM QUARTERLY RESULTS

This one is almost too general and too easy. But it's

amazing how much this is a problem for a lot of companies—typically public ones—and no one really talks about it.

Whole functions in the organization often exist just to be able to accurately and intelligently report results to Wall Street or other investors. It's often a scramble and a nightmare just to prepare for the report and the conversation each quarter.

THE QBR NIGHTMARE

I have a friend who works with a company where they have to do quarterly business reviews with investors. My friend regularly shrinks in her chair, shakes her head, and groans a loud "Uuuggghh!" any time anyone brings up the QBR.

According to her, it takes a team of more than ten people (mostly high-level management, which she is) more than two weeks of all-day work (and very long days at that—much longer than a typical day) to prepare for a one-hour phone call each quarter.

And the stress for everyone involved is crazy because of the need to present the company in the best light no matter what—even when results are not good. She says that it's very normal for the team that works on the QBR to get less than six hours of sleep per night during the process. And if her friends or family contact her during that time, she either ignores them or just responds with a text that says, "QBR."

It would be understandable if this process happened when the company first started reporting results or something like that and then got better over time. But it hasn't. It's been going on for years in the same way.

IGNORING YOUR DISEASE AND MAKING FAKE PROGRESS

Certainly reporting short-term results is not always all bad. But, apart from nightmare preparation stories, when short-term results are the hard focus for everyone, this causes companies to do things that seem like progress but really don't make sense.

In an effort to get good short-term results, and because they are afraid to not hit the numbers in a quarter or two, companies will avoid long-term investments (like replacing legacy technology) that they desperately need but will take longer to return. This is the same as ignoring a disease you have. You may get away with it for awhile, but eventually it will catch up with you.

Once company leaders find out that short-term performance is not good, there is often a scramble to explain why and come up with a bunch of short-term initiatives that will fix the numbers ASAP. This is very often the reason for the "hot new thing" that everyone is always trying to chase—or for the "flavor of the month" culture that takes hold in the company and causes everyone to not do their best because they know that next month everything will change again.

Usually these short-term initiatives displace smarter longer-term goals that have already been decided and that everyone in the company agrees are beneficial. They send all the departments into a distracting tailspin since everyone now needs to refocus on the "new initiatives" that now have high priority but clearly no one thought were that important earlier and are just a reaction to poor numbers. This process is often a "rinse and repeat" every quarter, since it's often hard to predict whether numbers can be made or not.

It's certainly bad to constantly add more initiatives each quarter on top of company goals. A bad variation of this is when companies change their goals throughout the year, whether overall goals or goals for a particular department or function. As with the flavor of the month, no one really knows what's expected of them, and they know it will likely change anyway. So there's no real effort except to "stay off the radar."

Not to mention, it's hard for most companies of any size to pivot so quickly. I've worked with companies of all sizes. Even small, highly entrepreneurial companies can have trouble being that nimble. As the company gets larger, doing so becomes even harder.

All these reactions by the organization are made by the "emotional brain." But we all know that true greatness, value, and strength for organizations comes from strategic planning and other rational brain functions, not from the emotional brain.

Ignoring your disease won't make it go away. Doing a bunch of activities that might make you feel good but don't cure your disease won't help for long either.

REACTING TO THE COMPETITION

Whatever the competition does often represents a shiny object that, like an email pop-up, is both very in-your-face visible and incredibly tempting to chase. In lieu of focusing on driving customer value, companies often only react to whatever their competitors do, especially if they see a good financial opportunity.

There are countless examples of this. For example, in the hospitality industry, if one major player decides to change its cancellation policy (or something similar), the others will certainly follow suit relatively soon.

In the consumer products industry, when Apple creates the iPhone and the Apple Watch, suddenly there are many other companies creating very similar products.

Inherently, there is nothing wrong with reacting to the competition, especially if you work to build on what the competition has done. But most companies just look at it as a way to keep up. They do it from a position of being afraid that if they don't do the same thing, they will lose out on opportunity. While they may be right, they are often missing a bigger point—an opportunity to reinvent a service, product, or process to truly make it better and more valuable for customers.

Often the need to react quickly to a competitor is because of the short-term results focus vs. working only to make a difference in customers' lives. The two issues are very closely related.

Also, sometimes reacting to a competitor comes from a lack of creativity, a lack of better ideas, or a fear that by the time you really get something that makes a difference in someone's life, it will be obsolete, or someone will have come up with something better.

Additionally, sometimes you need cash flow and profit in the short term to be able to sustain investment in longer-term initiatives that will really make a difference.

TREATING CHASING SHINY OBJECTS

The companies that are what I call "the titans of the world" today—the ones that really could take over the world if they wanted to—Apple, Google, Microsoft, Facebook, Amazon, and a handful of others—do not focus at all on making quarterly numbers. Not that they don't want to. They do.

But they know that making the quarterly numbers does not come from trying to make the quarterly numbers. Rather, it comes from making products or providing services that make a difference in peoples' lives.

BE A SURGEON AND A PAIN MANAGEMENT DOCTOR

Ideally, your product or service completely eliminates some pain in a customer's life, or—as Marie Kondo says—"sparks joy" in their life (joy, of course, being the opposite of pain). In case it's somehow not possible to completely eliminate the customer's pain (though I'd often challenge that assumption), at least your product or service should help customers better manage their pain.

Think of yourself first as a surgeon whose job is to cut out or change something that's hurting your patient. Then, think of yourself as a pain management doctor whose goal is to minimize the pain your patients are feeling from their "chronic condition" called life.

As a tool to assess your customers' pain (with your existing products or services or with some issue you are thinking of solving) take a cue from medicine. If you've ever gone to the emergency room because you're in a lot of pain—or if you've ever had surgery and are in pain from that—one of the first questions you will be asked is: on a scale of zero to ten, how bad is the pain?

Zero, of course, is no pain at all. Ten is the worst pain you've ever had in your life. This scale is universally understood.

It's so simple and effective that you don't even need to be able to read to use it. Hospitals display this pain scale in many places where doctors, nurses, or other providers will ask patients about their pain. And it always includes a diagram of faces that people can point to if they can't read.

Make sure to keep the focus on eliminating pain from the customer experience. Prioritize fixing the things that cause your customers the most pain. The titans of the world know that as long as they keep the focus on improving the world or improving peoples' lives, the quarterly numbers will happen.

FOCUS ON THE FUTURE

If the quarterly numbers don't happen for the titans, it's usually because they have strategically decided not to worry about them and are focusing on the long-term instead. Jeff Bezos, CEO of Amazon, said it brilliantly at the Economic Club of Washington, D.C. in September 2018: "All of our senior executives [at Amazon] operate the same way I do. They work in the future. They live in the future. None of the people who report to me should really be focused on the current quarter. Right now, I'm working on a quarter that's gonna reveal itself in 2021 sometime. And that's what you need to be doing. You need to be out...two or three years in advance."

While it's okay to look at the landscape and see what the competition is doing, resist the temptation to just follow. If you do follow, make it a short-term fix that will set the stage for something bigger. And definitely make sure that your short-term fix doesn't take up so many resources that you don't prioritize getting to the root of the issue and reinventing it.

REFOCUS YOUR MISSION

To stop Chasing Shiny Objects requires a clear vision and mission. This should come from what your company's purpose is and what differentiates you from the competition. If you don't have a crystal clear picture of what pain you're trying to eliminate for your customers (or what joy you're trying to spark in them), as well as what differentiates you (or how you want to be differentiated), first spend time figuring those things out and clarifying them.

Look again at your company's mission or vision statement. Does it specifically speak to the pain you want to eliminate or the joy you want to bring to your customers? If not, it probably needs to be changed and clarified.

Here are some diagnostic questions to ask about your mission statement. If you answer yes to one or more of these questions, take some time to refocus your mission.

- Is your mission statement only about your company and what you intend to do (e.g., provide X products or offer Y services) instead of speaking to what problem you will make disappear for your customers?

- Is it too generic such that it could apply to any company (e.g., to "enable everyone to be great")?

- Is it full of corporate jargon (e.g., "maximizing shareholder value" or "operating in value chains")?

- Does it have language that's related to your strategy or contain elements of your strategy (e.g., offering low prices or partnering with other companies)?

- Does it include anything about the benefits or results your company will get (e.g., "value for employees and shareholders")?

- Is it more than one sentence?

On the other hand, let's look at what a mission or vision statement should be. Your mission statement needs to be:

- **About the outcome for your customers**, not the outcome for your company. Certainly, it should not be something obvious and generic like "maximizing shareholder value." Everyone knows your company wants to do that. You don't need to say it in your mission statement.

  Doing so just makes you sound like you're either beating a dead horse, that you don't really believe in your mission, or that you're only trying to please investors and don't really care about customers. Best case is that it dilutes the strength of an otherwise good mission.

- **Applicable only to your company,** not everyone or any company. Be specific about what customers you are serving. The customers you mention in your mission statement can be relatively broad while still being specific (e.g., "professionals"). But your mission statement should only say that your customers are "everyone" if you really are that big and really are for everyone.

- **Simple, clear, memorable, and inspiring.** Use simple, clear words. Not corporate jargon. You may want to have marketing people help you here—or at least someone who is good with words. Just remember that complicated mission statements are bad, so don't get too caught up. Be honest, direct, simple, and real.

As examples of this, let's look at a few very good mission statements.

VERY GOOD MISSION STATEMENT	COMPANY
We save people money so they can live better.	Walmart
To connect the world's professionals to make them more productive and successful.	LinkedIn
To give everyone the power to create and share ideas and information instantly, without barriers.	Twitter
To organize the world's information and make it universally accessible and useful.	Google
To improve its customers' financial lives so profoundly, they couldn't imagine going back to the old way.	Intuit
To develop drugs to address significant unmet medical needs.	Genentech
To help people around the world plan and have the perfect trip.	TripAdvisor
To make a contribution to the world by making tools for the mind that advance humankind.	Apple (1980)

Notice how these mission statements vividly describe or imply what pain the company will cure for their customers. They contain no jargon or elements of strategy. They are simple, clear, and memorable. And they are only one sentence.

Your mission statement should help you make decisions, big and small. It should help you avoid Chasing Shiny Objects that don't ease your customers' pain or greatly improve their lives in the way you need to. It should help you quickly know if adding a particular product or service really is something you should do or not. It should even help you and your employees make simple decisions like: should you raise the price of X product by ten dollars?

If you have good products or services, you can have a very successful company with a bad mission statement. But once a company has financial challenges, watch out.

Often companies that have financial problems also have bad mission statements that no one really understands or cares about. As such, it's hard for company leaders (or anyone, really) to know what decision is most consistent with the company's true mission and the problems you're really trying to solve in your customers' lives. And that frequently leads to Chasing Shiny Objects.

STRUCTURE YOUR DISCIPLINE

You need discipline to stop Chasing Shiny Objects. Discipline is often associated with a person's character. While it's true that some people may be more naturally disciplined than others, remember Geary Rummler: "When you put good people up against a broken system, the broken system wins almost every time."

This means that in order to build discipline into your company, you need to put something in place structurally and ensure it has the environment to grow. Focus on the situation first, not just the people.

This doesn't have to be hard or complicated. But you need to do it. For example, perhaps it requires a quarterly, semi-annual, or annual meeting to see what the biggest problems are that people complain about, what the competition seems to be doing, and where there are gaps that need to be filled.

This should certainly be part of the goal-setting process each year, and that may be enough by itself.

Once these structures are established for how to monitor the competitive and market landscape and assess the major customer pains (or opportunities for joy), then the "laser focus" should be on how to fix those issues. Period. Anything else is a distraction.

LOAD YOUR ENVIRONMENT WITH TRUE BELIEVERS

With all I've said in this book about fostering an effective environment for your company and not relying so much on people's internal characteristics, let's not forget about you and the executive team. We need to make sure your situation and environment enable you to lead your company to be its best. To do that, we need to talk about your investors and your board.

There's a saying in the nonfiction publishing business:

"It's better to have 1,000 true believers than 10,000 followers." The same is true for your investors and your board.

Although it may seem more difficult, you must make sure you are working with the right investors and board in order to set your company up for true long-term success. Be transparent with potential investors about the fact that you're in this for the long haul and that people looking for short-term returns may not be the best investors because what you're doing will take some time.

Although you may turn off some investors (or analysts if you're publicly traded), those who remain will be the true believers—the ones who share your philosophy and will help you best in your company's journey. Without this, and especially if you have investors that are heavily focused on short-term results, it will always be difficult for you to jump off that hamster wheel and cure this critical flaw.

As we've seen in this chapter, Chasing Shiny Objects is another flaw that causes lots of other problems and critical flaws downstream.

KEY TAKEAWAYS FROM THIS CHAPTER

- Don't be distracted by short-term focus or competitors.

- Be a surgeon and a pain management doctor. Keep the focus on making your customers' lives better by eliminating pain and "sparking joy."

- Clarify your company's vision and mission to reflect how you eliminate pain or "spark joy."

- Use structure to build discipline in your company.

- Work with only "true believer" investors.

AN OUNCE OF PREVENTION

You've spent good time reading through this book, learning about the critical flaws in your company and how to diagnose, treat, and cure them. There's a lot you understand—hopefully more than you ever have. You're feeling generally confident, and you have a plan.

But you're still a little worried. What happens if you spend a lot of time and money, and the flaws don't go away? Or what happens if you fix the flaws, and they come back? Then what?

As the final chapter in your journey, let's talk about prevention. After all, an ounce of prevention is worth a pound of cure, right?

As I said in the introduction of this book, if you put effort into fixing the flaws and they don't go away, perhaps you missed one of the key steps to treating one or more of them. More likely you probably didn't treat all the flaws. Or you tried to do so too quickly, without patience and mindfulness. To prevent this from happening—and also to prevent a recurrence of one or more of the flaws—remember to treat all the flaws and take the time to do it right.

To help with prevention, there are a couple of simple tactics.

THE REGULAR CHECKUP

In our personal lives, we go to the doctor once a year to make sure there's nothing wrong with us. In any business, we constantly audit our computers to make sure there are no viruses or malware that would affect their performance or cause harm. The same premise should inform the regular checkup regarding your company's critical flaws.

In a very real way, these types of organizational flaws are as damaging as a data breach caused by an undetected virus or hack. They don't always feel as acute as a data breach, perhaps. But they likely do much more expansive damage that lasts longer.

Think of a chronic medical condition versus an acute illness like the flu. While the flu may get a lot of attention, chronic hypertension quietly kills many more people. Same thing with the critical flaws from an organizational perspective.

You wouldn't think twice about seeing your doctor for your annual physical—especially if you have previously had a serious or life-threatening illness. So why not apply the same principle to your company? To make it really easy, schedule your critical flaws audit a day or so after your physical. And use the Company Symptom Questionnaire template on my website to help you.

THE TRAUMA COMMITTEE

Many hospitals have a great process that comes from horrible roots. The trauma committee is the group of physicians in the hospital that are responsible for reviewing all of the really bad cases that come into the hospital (gunshot wounds, car accidents, you name it). Their goal is to examine all these cases to determine what went well, what went wrong, and what to do better next time. From these committees have come numerous improved processes designed to avoid flaws that literally kill people, as well as to prevent future trauma victims from dying whenever trauma strikes.

This is a great concept for the business world. And it's the perfect place to make sure you're paying attention to the critical flaws.

If you already have committees that get together to do a "postmortem" on an initiative that didn't work out, make sure you address the critical flaws discussed in this book, as well as those specific to the initiative. Maybe it wasn't that the product, service, or strategy was bad—but, rather, that your company had too many flaws to adapt and support it.

If you don't have anything like this in your company, consider creating it. You don't have to call it a "trauma committee" if that concerns you. You could call it a SWAT team or whatever you want—as long as you do it properly.

The key to doing this post-game assessment properly is to involve a key leader from every process of the business and meet regularly (e.g., every month) to discuss any organizational or customer problems that may have come up. Just remember that the point of the trauma committee is prevention, not finger-pointing.

If you get to a point where you don't really have any major problems on a regular basis, that's great. Shift the focus to continuous improvement, thinking more about what's on the horizon, what you could do to bring extra joy to your customers, or what additional pains your customers have. Or stop having the meeting if you want.

Just don't forget that whenever there are problems, the

trauma committee needs to be there to help the company learn (without blaming) and prevent those problems from happening again.

CONCLUSION

Before you go off and execute your plan to cure all the critical flaws in your company, take one last look at your plan to make sure it's complete. To help ensure you address all the flaws properly, here are the key takeaways from each chapter.

POLITICS

There are many different kinds of politics. Don't pretend that politics will go away if you ignore them. You must deal with them. Treat politics like a bad marriage and go to "counseling." Clear processes, standards, and goals, as well as a well-designed organization, are also necessary for eliminating politics.

BLIND SPOTS

Listen to the complainers (perception is reality). Do solid

self-reflection yourself and at all levels in the organization about what you and your competitors do that sucks and everyone hates. Prioritize removing friction, bureaucracy, politics, and worthless processes. Use anticipation and details to ease your customers' pain, make their lives better, personalize their experiences, and surprise and delight them. It will build lasting loyalty and grow your revenue. Write "great last chapters" like Danny Meyer.

SCAPEGOATING

Consider causality vs. correlation before placing blame and treating. Otherwise, you could give the wrong treatment, which, like in medicine, is bad. There is a sliding scale from neutral/bad to really awful. Look to all inputs in the environment before blaming people or other scapegoats. In addition to having a dedicated change management process, focus on peoples' emotions and on "shaping the path" in the work environment to enable a change to take hold and succeed.

UNCLEAR GOALS

Make sure everyone agrees on KPIs and how to evaluate success or failure, as well as what success looks like. Be as precise and numerical as possible when establishing goals. Share goals across the company for everyone and eliminate siloed goals.

DOING TOO MUCH

Stop doing too many initiatives at once. Host a "vital few retreat" at the beginning of the year to prioritize no more than three to five initiatives. Focus everyone in the company on the vital few. Stick to your guns and don't stray from the vital few.

DYSFUNCTIONAL INFRASTRUCTURE

Dysfunctional infrastructure is often the deepest root cause of poor performance in your company, but few people think of it or have the courage to truly address it. Redesign all parts of your company infrastructure to eliminate friction and support cross-functional collaboration that improves the lives of your customers and employees.

NO SOPs

Stop making excuses for not being process-focused. Take the time to create optimal processes and document them properly. Repurpose your process documentation throughout your company to ensure common language, alignment, consistency, and scalability.

FIXING THE UNFIXABLE

Stop focusing too much on underperformance even

though it is tempting to do so. Engineer the performance curve to be "right and tight."

LEGACY TECHNOLOGY

Replacing legacy technology is SHIT-E. There's a risk it will fail. But you should do it. Hire more programmers/ developers/coders. The faster they move, the faster you move. Replacing legacy technology is an opportunity to become a disruptor, leapfrog your competitors, thrill your customers, and potentially change the world.

CHASING SHINY OBJECTS

Don't be distracted by short-term focus or competitors. Be a surgeon and a pain management doctor. Keep the focus on making your customers' lives better (or peoples' lives better) by eliminating pain and "sparking joy." Clarify your company's vision and mission to reflect how you eliminate pain or "spark joy." Use structure to build discipline in your company. Work with only "true believer" investors.

FINAL THOUGHTS

Now that you've got your action plan complete and you're prepared for how to prevent the critical flaws from coming back later, it's time to pull the trigger. You know what to do. You can do it. You will do it.

Be patient. Take your time. Work through the process.

Know that even though you are at the top of your company, you are not alone. There are lots of tools on my website, www.joshrovner.com, to help you. There will be lots of support available to you along the way from many different people, including your team and the people in your company.

Keep me posted on your progress. I'd love to hear about your successes and challenges. You're always welcome to email me at josh@joshrovner.com.

A friend of mine once said that from what he sees in the world today—and for the foreseeable future—the evolution of our society is going to come from business and the business world.

Given your position in your company, you have a unique opportunity to cure your company's critical flaws and fix its performance. By doing so—and by running your company in a way that's not only better for financial performance but also for the people (including yourself!)—you have the opportunity to help our society, and humanity in general, evolve for the better.

Accordingly, I will leave you with a few of the inspirational words of President George H.W. Bush from the handwritten letter that he wrote to President Bill Clinton and left in the Resolute Desk in the Oval Office at the White House in 1993. Because now they apply to you, too.

"...don't let the critics discourage you or push you off course...Your success is now our country's success. I am rooting hard for you."

ACKNOWLEDGMENTS

There are so many people I want to acknowledge. I hate having to narrow it down because I'm afraid to leave someone off. But here we go:

Tucker Max—Thank you for believing in me and in this book; for giving me great guidance; and for taking my writing and thinking game to the next level. Thank you for helping me understand the greater purpose and the ripple effect. I have learned a lot from you.

Emily Gindlesparger—I am beyond grateful for all the times where you quickly "unstuck" me.

Hal Clifford—Thank you for your experience, guidance, and honesty. I am extremely grateful for how well you both pushed and supported me. This book is better because of you. I am a better writer because of you.

Erin Tyler, Cindy Curtis, and the Scribe cover design team—Thank you for putting up with all my revisions and creating a phenomenal cover that I never would have come up with on my own!

Natalie Aboudaoud—Thank you for keeping me on track, for your advocacy, and for answering my many questions about the process.

Everyone else at Scribe Media—You are an amazing group of people, and I am honored and humbled to have worked with you. You have definitely fulfilled your mission with me. Thank you for unlocking my wisdom.

My fellow Scribe authors—I am honored to be part of our community. I'm lucky to know all of you and to consider you friends, given all your talents, experiences, and strengths.

Paul Elliott—Thank you for being the spark that started me on this journey and for helping me see the way so clearly. I am lucky to have met you and to have had you as a mentor in this arena all these years. I am also extremely grateful for all the times you encouraged me to write and publish. I would not have written this book if it weren't for your support and enthusiasm.

Mark Schor—You have changed my life in so many ways and helped me through some of the most difficult times in my life. Your ability to flip a switch in me is remarkable. You are a wise man and a mensch.

Jill Vershum—Thank you for helping me find my core, my presence, and my power.

Rozanne Gold—Thank you for your valuable insights and experience, your brilliance with words and titles at just the right moments, and your thoughtful listening.

All my former leaders and teams—You have all inspired me, and I have learned from all of you. I am very grateful.

Jeana Pullen—Thank you for being a friend. I don't know what I would have done without you.

Todd, Hammond, Pete—I love you guys.

Mom and Dad—Thank you for your unconditional love and support. You are the best parents I could ever imagine. It's impossible to put into words how grateful I am to have you as my parents. I love you both so much!

Noelia—I love you more. I am so lucky to have been married to you all these years. You are a perfect balance to me, and I would not be where I am today if I had not met you. Thank you for all the times you listened to me during this process and for all the times you listen to me about everything—even when I ramble on and on!

Rebecca—You are the best daughter ever. It's impossible to find words to describe how much I love you and how proud I am of you. You are kind, loving, funny, and strong. Every day you make me smile and laugh, and you warm my heart. You are a superstar, and I know you are going to do great things in this world. I am beyond lucky to have you in my life!

ABOUT THE AUTHOR

JOSH ROVNER has more than twenty years of experience as a leader and consultant, working with all levels of small to large corporations to grow their revenues and improve their performance. Josh leads change and transforms businesses by communicating clearly about complex subjects, designing effective processes, and developing and coaching people. Josh received his bachelor of science in communications, summa cum laude, from Boston University, and his master of management in hospitality from Cornell University. He lives in Dallas, Texas.

www.ingramcontent.com/pod-product-compliance
Lightning Source LLC
Chambersburg PA
CBHW031843200326
41597CB00012B/250